Kibana 8.x – A Quick Start Guide to Data Analysis

Learn about data exploration, visualization, and dashboard building with Kibana

Krishna Shah

Kibana 8.x – A Quick Start Guide to Data Analysis

Associate Group Product Manager: Kaustubh Manglurkar

Associate Publishing Product Manager: Heramb Bhavsar

Book Project Manager: Kirti Pisat

Senior Editor: Tiksha Lad

Technical Editor: Rahul Limbachiya

Copy Editor: Safis Editing

Proofreader: Safis Editing

Indexer: Pratik Shirodkar

Production Designer: Joshua Misquitta

Senior DevRel Marketing Coordinator: Nivedita Singh

First published: February 2024
Production reference: 2280224

Published by Packt Publishing Ltd.
Grosvenor House
11 St Paul's Square
Birmingham
B3 1RB, UK.

ISBN 978-1-80323-216-4

www.packtpub.com

For Ashok Shah,

In the library of your memory, I shelve this work, papa. May the whispers of data echo your passion for stories, and may you be proud of the chapters I write with your unseen hand, guiding me still.

- Krishna Shah

Contributors

About the author

Krishna Shah is a data architect from Melbourne, Australia with 9+ years of experience, and she knows how to make data work. She's been an official trainer for Elasticsearch and Kibana, crafting the courses that empower people to unlock the secrets of data. Prior to that, she worked for a start-up in India as the data engineer behind building and maintaining data engineering pipelines, then transforming that raw information into stunning visuals and insights using Kibana and other data engineering technologies. Today, she's an advocate, a mentor, and a bridge-builder, inviting everyone to find their own rhythm in the data's dance. Whether you're a novice or seasoned analyst, brace yourself for her infectious enthusiasm and knack for making the driest of datasets sing!

About the reviewer

Peter Steenbergen is a principal solutions architect at Elastic. Peter was one of the first people to receive the Elastic Certified Professional of the Year award and has many years of experience in building solutions with the Elastic Stack. He enjoys helping people in the community to solve their search and observability use cases leveraging the Elastic Stack. This could be through in-company training, knowledge-sharing workshops, or on-site consultative sessions. If he's not behind a computer, you can find him riding his mountain bike, running through the woods, or, with his latest hobby, playing on a padel court.

Table of Contents

Part 2: Visualizations in Kibana

4

How About We Visualize?   37

5

Powering Visualizations with Near Real-Time Updates   63

Part 3: Analytics on a Dashboard

6

Data Analysis with Machine Learning   81

7

Graph Visualization   97

8

Finally, the Dashboard   107

Part 4: Querying on Kibana and Advanced Concepts

9

ES|QL and Advanced Kibana Concepts   123

10

Query DSL and Management through Kibana   143

Preface

Seven years ago, I stumbled upon Elasticsearch – not as a technical instructor but as a wide-eyed data detective. It was after that I discovered Kibana; I was captivated by its ability to transform cold, numerical figures into vibrant stories, each query a brushstroke painting the canvas of insights. As I delved deeper, its power to democratize data analysis, making it accessible not just to elite statisticians but to anyone with a curious mind, ignited a passion within me.

This passion led me to the world of official Kibana 8 training, where I witnessed firsthand the transformative impact it had on individuals and organizations. But a nagging feeling persisted – the existing resources, while comprehensive, felt like dense tomes for seasoned explorers, leaving newcomers lost in the wilderness of data.

That's where the seed of this book was sown. I envisioned a guide that didn't just explain the "what" and "how" of Kibana but also captured the "why." I wanted to translate the magic I saw in classrooms onto the page, making Kibana not just a tool but a bridge to a world of data-driven discovery.

Researching this book wasn't just about combing through documentation and tutorials; it was about reliving the journey of my students. I revisited the challenges they faced, the "aha!" moments they experienced, and the questions that lingered long after the training ended. I talked to data enthusiasts, industry experts, and fellow Kibana instructors, gathering their insights and weaving them into a tapestry of practical knowledge.

Each chapter became a brushstroke on the canvas of my vision. I crafted exercises that mirrored real-world scenarios, using familiar datasets to make the learning process relatable and engaging. I translated complex concepts into digestible language, using humor and anecdotes to keep the journey as enjoyable as it is informative.

This book is more than just a compilation of Kibana functionalities; it's an invitation to embark on a data-driven adventure. It's for the curious mind, the aspiring analyst, or anyone who wants to unlock the secrets hidden within their data. It's my way of sharing the magic I witnessed, igniting that spark of data passion in others, and guiding them on their own journey from data novice to empowered data detective.

Ready to transform raw data into captivating stories? This book is your Rosetta Stone, unlocking the power of Kibana 8.x. Delve into Discover, craft visual symphonies with dashboards, and unveil hidden patterns with **Machine Learning (ML)** and **Time Series Visual Builder (TSVB)**. Master ES|QL's precise sculpting, bend data with dynamic runtime fields, and learn to manage your domain with ease. Let Kibana be your data maestro, conducting insights with elegance and precision. Now, turn the page and let the analysis begin!

Who this book is for

Calling all data curious, analysis enthusiasts, and visualization voyagers! Whether you're a seasoned data wrangler or a wide-eyed newbie, this book welcomes you with open arms (and dashboards!). This book is your launchpad to unlock the power of Kibana, the interactive data visualization platform that transforms raw numbers into captivating stories. If you're hungry to explore hidden patterns, unearth trends from your data, and paint vibrant pictures of insights, then this guide is your compass. Whether you're a marketer charting customer journeys, an IT whiz troubleshooting server logs, or a scientist diving into research findings, Kibana has a seat for you at its analysis table. So, ditch the spreadsheets and dive into the dynamic world of data visualization – we'll start with baby steps and soon have you dancing with dashboards.

What this book covers

Chapter 1, Introduction to Kibana, unlocks the power of Kibana by diving into the vibrant world of data visualization. This chapter lays the foundation, introducing you to Kibana – an interactive platform that transforms raw data into captivating stories. You'll learn its purpose, its core features, and why it's the go-to tool for data explorers. Moreover, you will be guided through the exciting process of setting up your own Kibana environment, from installing and configuring the software to connecting it to your data source.

Chapter 2, Creating Data Views and Introducing Spaces, unlocks two powerful features that elevate your analysis game. You'll be guided through crafting tailored data views and personalized dashboards that focus on specific aspects of your data, letting you zero in on critical insights by creating a data view that helps you select and work on a specific type of data in Kibana. Then, you will be prepared to explore the revolutionary concept of Kibana spaces. This chapter unlocks doors to efficient data sharing, streamlined workflows, and a world where collaboration takes center stage.

Chapter 3, Discovering Data through Discover, equips you with the tools to explore your datasets like a seasoned detective, sifting through raw information to uncover hidden patterns and unveil compelling insights. You'll master the powerful search bar, unleashing precise queries to pinpoint specific data points. You'll learn the Kibana Query Language to search through your data and also create filters. You'll see how Discover helps us explore the data before you begin your analytics journey on your dataset.

Chapter 4, How About We Visualize?, unlocks the visual language of data in Kibana, transforming cold numbers into captivating stories. Forget static spreadsheets – here, you'll wield diverse charts and graphs like magic wands, revealing hidden patterns and trends within your information. You'll get to explore the power of bar charts, line graphs, and heatmaps, learning how each Lens editing tool paints a unique picture of your data's essence. You'll master the art of selecting the right visual for the job, ensuring your insights resonate with clarity and impact.

Chapter 5, Powering Visualizations with Near-Real-Time Updates, dives into the exciting world of near real-time data visualization with TSVB. You'll learn to craft visualizations that update seamlessly as new information flows in, revealing hidden patterns and trends as they unfold. You get to explore TSVB's powerful features, such as expressions, aggregations, and bucket scripting, empowering you to transform raw data into captivating stories that update with the pulse of your live systems.

Chapter 6, Data Analysis with Machine Learning, will delve into the exciting realm of ML within Kibana. Imagine using data patterns and algorithms to uncover hidden insights, predict trends, and automate anomaly detection. You'll get to explore tools such as anomaly detection, outlier analysis, and even supervised learning, all within your familiar Kibana interface. It is a powerful fusion of data analysis and ML, unlocking a whole new layer of understanding and actionable insights from your data.

Chapter 7, Graph Visualization, will help you learn to untangle the web of your data! This chapter equips you with the power of graphs to unveil hidden connections, trace relationships, and spot patterns lurking beneath the surface of numbers.

Chapter 8, Finally, the Dashboard, teaches you how to transform raw data into visually captivating dashboards that tell a clear and compelling story. You will craft interactive layouts, weave together powerful visualizations, and apply custom filters to empower anyone to explore and understand your data with ease. This is where information comes alive, guiding informed decisions and sparking insightful conversations.

Chapter 9, ES|QL and Advanced Kibana Concepts, explores the power of data manipulation where you dive into ES|QL, crafting custom Elasticsearch queries to sculpt your insights. You will unleash runtime fields, dynamically generating data points for deeper analysis on the fly. Finally, you will master advanced Kibana settings to understand how to fine-tune your environment for maximum visual impact and intuitive exploration.

Chapter 10, Query DSL and Management through Kibana, takes a deep dive into the pulse of your data with Query DSL. You will craft precise searches, sculpt results, and bend information to your will. We'll explore Kibana's data management tools, keeping your information kingdom organized and secure. Prepare to master both precision and control, one query and setting at a time!

Disclaimer:

This book, *Kibana 8. x: A Quick Start Guide to Data Analysis*, is not sponsored, endorsed, or affiliated with Elastic NV ("Elastic") or any of its subsidiaries or affiliates. The contributors to this book are independent authors and are not acting on behalf of or as representatives of, Elastic in any capacity. The content of this book is solely the responsibility of the authors and does not necessarily reflect the views or opinions of Elastic. Elastic makes no representations or warranties of any kind, express or implied, regarding the accuracy, completeness, or timeliness of the content of this book.

To get the most out of this book

It is recommended to have a basic understanding of data. Familiarity with data types, structures, and concepts will ease navigation through Kibana's data manipulation tools.

Some SQL knowledge is useful. While not essential, basic SQL skills can come in handy for writing simple queries in ES|QL, Kibana's query language.

Conceptual know-how on downloading, installing, and configuring Kibana and working with YAML files is essential.

If you are using the digital version of this book, we advise you to type the code yourself or access the code from the book's GitHub repository (a link is available in the next section). Doing so will help you avoid any potential errors related to the copying and pasting of code.

Download the example code files

You can download the example code files for this book from GitHub at `https://github.com/PacktPublishing/Kibana-8.x-A-Quick-Start-Guide-to-Data-Analysis`. If there's an update to the code, it will be updated in the GitHub repository.

We also have other code bundles from our rich catalog of books and videos available at `https://github.com/PacktPublishing/`. Check them out!

Conventions used

There are a number of text conventions used throughout this book.

`Code in text`: Indicates code words in text, database table names, folder names, filenames, file extensions, pathnames, dummy URLs, user input, and Twitter handles. Here is an example: "For example, `GET _ml/info` will simply return the result of the current machine learning jobs on the cluster."

A block of code is set as follows:

```
GET _ml/memory/<node_id>/_stats
GET _ml/memory/_stats
```

Any command-line input or output is written as follows:

```
<iframe src="https://juxwycstgeesmshyp-xxxxxxxxxx.rp.strigo.io/
app/r/s/xAwTf" height="600" width="800"></iframe>
```

Bold: Indicates a new term, an important word, or words that you see on screen. For instance, words in menus or dialog boxes appear in **bold**. Here is an example: "Inside the **Documents** layer, select **data view/Index pattern** you wish to work on and the **Geospatial** field, and then click on **Add layer** at the bottom."

> Tips or important notes
> Appear like this.

Get in touch

Feedback from our readers is always welcome.

General feedback: If you have questions about any aspect of this book, email us at `customercare@packtpub.com` and mention the book title in the subject of your message.

Errata: Although we have taken every care to ensure the accuracy of our content, mistakes do happen. If you have found a mistake in this book, we would be grateful if you would report this to us. Please visit www.packtpub.com/support/errata and fill in the form.

Piracy: If you come across any illegal copies of our works in any form on the internet, we would be grateful if you would provide us with the location address or website name. Please contact us at copyright@packt.com with a link to the material.

If you are interested in becoming an author: If there is a topic that you have expertise in and you are interested in either writing or contributing to a book, please visit authors.packtpub.com.

Share your thoughts

Once you've read *Kibana 8.x: A Quick Start Guide to Data Analysis*, we'd love to hear your thoughts! Scan the QR code below to go straight to the Amazon review page for this book and share your feedback.

https://packt.link/r/1803232161

Your review is important to us and the tech community and will help us make sure we're delivering excellent quality content.

Download a free PDF copy of this book

Thanks for purchasing this book!

Do you like to read on the go but are unable to carry your print books everywhere?

Is your eBook purchase not compatible with the device of your choice?

Don't worry, now with every Packt book you get a DRM-free PDF version of that book at no cost.

Read anywhere, any place, on any device. Search, copy, and paste code from your favorite technical books directly into your application.

The perks don't stop there, you can get exclusive access to discounts, newsletters, and great free content in your inbox daily

Follow these simple steps to get the benefits:

1. Scan the QR code or visit the link below

https://packt.link/free-ebook/9781803232164

2. Submit your proof of purchase
3. That's it! We'll send your free PDF and other benefits to your email directly

Part 1:
Exploring Kibana

This part covers Kibana's core functionality: transforming raw data into captivating insights. We'll craft data views, which are customized lenses used to focus on specific data subsets. We will introduce you to spaces, which are collaborative containers for sharing and organizing dashboards. Finally, the **Discover** tab will become your playground, where queries unveil hidden patterns and trends, weaving data into stories that guide your decisions. Here, you also get equipped to explore, visualize, and understand the true power of Kibana in data exploration and discovery.

This part has the following chapters:

- *Chapter 1, Introduction to Kibana*
- *Chapter 2, Creating Data Views and Introducing Spaces*
- *Chapter 3, Discovering the Data through Discover*

1

Introduction to Kibana

Now is the time to kickstart our journey into the world of visualizing data. We are first going to start understanding the core concepts of Kibana, right from setting up, installing, and configuring to starting Kibana. We will also learn how Kibana acts as a window to your data stored in Elasticsearch. Kibana, being an open source application, is also a UI layer of Elastic Stack for visualizing and exploring data in Elasticsearch. It can also be used to manage the stack.

The following are the topics that we will cover in detail:

- Getting an overview of Kibana
- Understanding data integrations

Technical requirements

Kibana requires specific hardware specifications when installed on a server, which includes support for 64-bit operating systems. The installation process offers multiple package formats, such as `tar`, `deb`, `rpm`, and Docker. Kibana can be installed, configured, and started from an archive on Linux, macOS, or Windows.

The hardware requirements for Kibana may vary depending on the specific use-case requirements. However, it is generally recommended to allocate 1 GB to 2 GB of RAM and 2 CPUs for use cases involving PDF, CSV, and PNG reporting in Kibana.

Getting an overview of Kibana

Kibana is a powerful tool for data discovery, analysis, visualization, and security. It's designed for administrators, analysts, and business users to manage, monitor, and secure their Elastic Stack deployments. Kibana provides a comprehensive suite of features for searching, observing, and protecting data. It's easy to quickly find documents and uncover hidden insights, visualize results in charts, gauges, maps, graphs, and more, and combine them in a dashboard. Analysts can explore and analyze data with the help of Kibana's sophisticated query language, and administrators can manage and monitor the health of their Elastic Stack cluster.

It is a great tool for a wide range of use cases. For instance, it can be used to monitor website traffic, search log files for errors and anomalies, and even detect security vulnerabilities. It can also be used to analyze customer data for marketing campaigns, track events for compliance, and visualize the performance of a computer system.

Data analysis is a core functionality of Kibana. And the journey doesn't end there. We can use a variety of different graphs to slice our data, in order to bring out meaningful insights to our data that otherwise might be obscured. It is also important to understand that Kibana visualizations are built on top of Elasticsearch aggregations such as average, min, max, sum, percentiles, and bucket aggregations such as terms, histogram, date histogram, and so on. Depending on the need of the hour, one of these can be selected to depict the data in pictorial form. Once we have all we need on a visualization and we have a collection of them set up, we can then bring all of them together to create a comprehensive visualization called a dashboard. Dashboards give us a unified view of many different data points on a single page in order to make the best correlation and spot trends in datasets.

Installation

Kibana is a powerful data visualization platform used to create visualizations and dashboards of data stored within Elasticsearch. It is crucial to configure Kibana to operate with an Elasticsearch node that matches the same version. Kibana can be installed via several different methods depending on the operating system and environment. From the Kibana 6.0.0 version onward, Kibana is supporting 64-bit systems only.

One of the easiest ways to get started with Kibana is to download the `tar.gz` package for installation on Linux and Darwin. Firing up an Elastic Cloud deployment as a trial is also a great way to start getting familiar with Kibana. This can be done from `https://www.elastic.co/cloud`, which gives users a 15-day trial to deploy any type of data. For Docker use cases, the Docker images are available for download from the official Docker registry. For Debian and Ubuntu systems, the `deb` package can be used for installing Kibana. As a prerequisite, it is assumed that you have an Elasticsearch cluster installed, configured, and secured in order to generate the username and password that we will be using here to log in to Kibana.

Once the appropriate package has been downloaded, installation of Kibana is relatively straightforward. Here is a list of ways to do it:

- For Linux and Darwin, Kibana can be installed by unzipping the `tar.gz` package and running the Kibana binary
- For Linux-based systems, we can use the `deb` package, which can be installed with the `dpkg` command
- Installing Kibana as a Docker container requires the image to be downloaded and run with the `docker run` command

- Finally, the rpm package can be installed on Red Hat, **SUSE Linux Enterprise Server (SLES)**, openSUSE, and other RPM-based systems with the rpm command

Once Kibana has been installed, the Kibana configuration file can be edited, and the service can be started. This will allow the Kibana instance to connect to the Elasticsearch node and begin creating visualizations and dashboards. It is important to ensure that Kibana is configured to run against an Elasticsearch node of the same version to ensure compatibility.

So far, we have learned and explored different ways to install Kibana. Next, we will look into configuring Kibana through its YML file.

Configuration

Configuring Kibana is a relatively simple process. It is important to know where the kibana.yml file is located as it is the main configuration file for Kibana. The Kibana.yml file is located in the main directory of the kibana folder. Depending on how Kibana was installed, the location of the file will be different.

Once the kibana.yml file is located, it can be used to configure a variety of settings. The default host and port settings configure Kibana to run on localhost:5601, but this can be changed to allow remote users to connect. SSL can also be enabled, and other options can be set. Environment variables can also be injected into the configuration using ${MY_ENV_VAR}. After any changes are made to the kibana.yml file, it is important to save the changes and restart the Kibana server for the changes to take effect.

Running Kibana

Starting Kibana is a straightforward process. Here are the steps for it:

1. To begin, open the command line and navigate to the directory containing the Kibana executable file (bin/kibana).
2. Then, type in ./bin/kibana and press *Enter*. This will start Kibana and generate a unique link in your terminal. You'll need to click this link in order to open Kibana in your browser.
3. Once you see Kibana has loaded in the browser, we will need to log in to Kibana with the username and password that was created when you secured your Elasticsearch cluster.

Stopping Kibana is a simple process as well. All you must do is press *Ctrl* + *C* in the terminal where Kibana is running. This will stop Kibana, and the instance will no longer be running. However, it's important to note that any data or settings that were changed while running Kibana will not be saved unless you take the necessary steps to save them before stopping Kibana.

Now that we know how to kickstart Kibana, the next step is to explore how to add data to our storage – Elasticsearch.

Understanding data integrations

When it comes to adding data to Elasticsearch, there are multiple ways to do it.

The easiest and simplest method would be to add the sample data available on Kibana's home page by clicking on **Try sample data** as shown in the following figure:

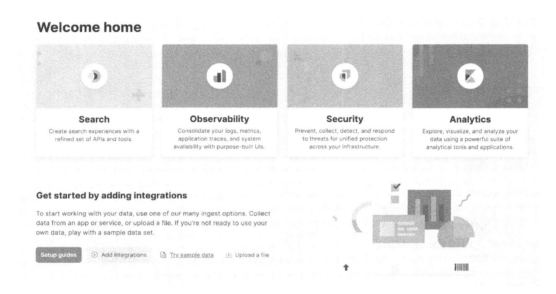

Figure 1.1 – Image shows the page of Kibana where you have options to add sample data

This shows a **Sample data** screen where a dropdown can be found through an **Other datasets** link. There are currently three options to choose from:

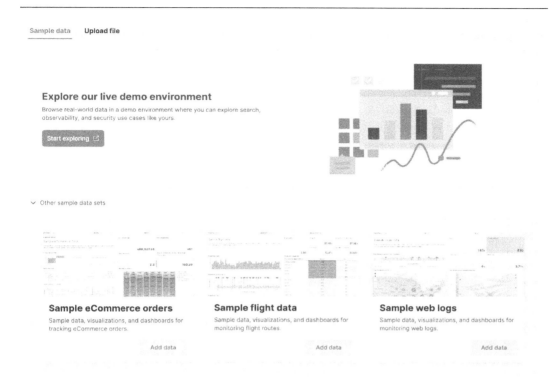

Figure 1.2 – The page of Kibana where you have options to add sample data

Next, an easy option to explore data would be to add the data through the **Upload file** option, where a log file or delimited CSV, TSV, or JSON file up to the size of 100 MB can be uploaded. This value can be configured up to 1 GB in the **Advanced settings** section of Kibana:

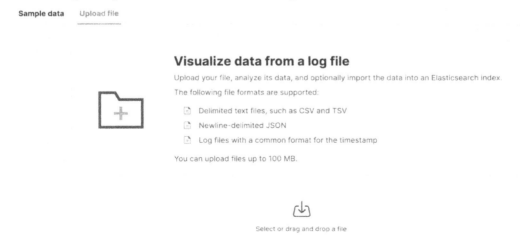

Figure 1.3 – Using the load feature to add the sample data

Other options to add data can be through Elastic Agents by using one of the many integrations that are available for most services and platforms in the market. Integrations can be navigated on the home screen of Kibana, as shown in the following screenshot:

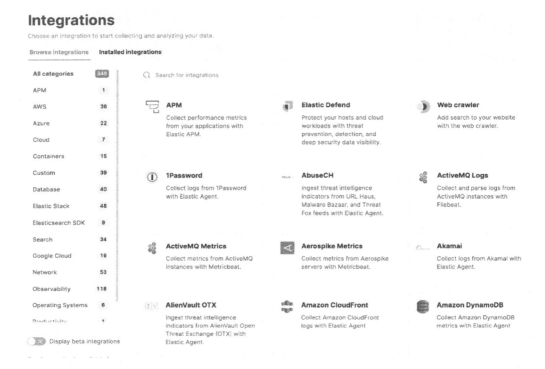

Figure 1.4 – The Integrations page of Kibana with options to add an integration based on our data sources

We can also use the Elasticsearch API to add data to an Elasticsearch index. The API offers several methods for adding data, including the `index`, `create`, and `bulk` methods.

Let us understand each of these ahead:

- `index`: The `index` method is used to create or update a document in the index. It requires specifying the index, type, and ID of the document, along with the data to be added. Here is an example of it:

```
POST /my_index/_doc/1
{"name": "John Doe",
 "age": 30,
"occupation": "Software Engineer"
}
```

- create: The create method is like the index method, but it only creates a new document if it does not already exist. If a document with the specified ID already exists, it will return an error.

  Here's an example:

  ```
  PUT /my_index/_create/1
  {
    "name": "John Doe",
  "age": 30,
  "occupation": "Software Engineer"
    }
  ```

- bulk: The bulk method allows you to add multiple documents in a single request. This can improve performance when adding large amounts of data.

  Here's an example:

  ```
  POST /my_index/_bulk
    {"index": {"_id": "1"} } {"name": "John Doe", "age": 30,
  "occupation": "Software Engineer"}
    {"index" : {"_id" : "2"} {"name": "Jane Smith", "age": 25,
  "occupation": "Marketing Specialist"}
  ```

In addition to the API, there are also client libraries available for various programming languages that provide a more convenient way to interact with Elasticsearch and add data. These libraries often have built-in methods or functions for adding data to an index.

Another popular method for adding data to Elasticsearch is using **Logstash**, which is a data processing pipeline that allows you to ingest and transform data before it is added to Elasticsearch. Logstash supports various input plugins for collecting data from different sources, such as file inputs, database inputs, and network inputs. Once the data is collected, it can be processed and enriched using various filter plugins and then sent to Elasticsearch for indexing.

With this, we conclude our discussion on data integrations.

Summary

In this chapter, we studied in detail how Kibana can be installed from scratch, configured, and started on platforms. We also saw how there can be numerous ways to add data to an Elasticsearch cluster.

In the next chapter, we will be learning the next step in exploring Kibana – data views. We will learn how data can be navigated in Kibana by creating data views and how spaces help us much better organize our Kibana environment.

2

Creating Data Views and Introducing Spaces

If you've been wondering when we will really start working on Kibana, now is the time!

In the last chapter, we explored the installation, configuration, and starting/stopping of Kibana, along with looking at different ways to add data. Now is the time to start taking a deep dive into how we explore our data in Kibana. The first and foremost step is to create a data view (it was called an **index pattern** in older versions of Kibana) through Kibana's UI page. We will see the step-by-step process of how to create them, explore them for fields and field mappings (data types), and make the best sense of our data.

Here are the topics we'll now start exploring:

- Exploring data views
- Creating spaces
- Understanding saved objects in Kibana

Technical requirements

As per the basic requirements, we assume that you have data ingested in the cluster and that Kibana is set up on the nodes of (any) environment (cloud or local).

Exploring data views

Data views are structures that help us navigate Elasticsearch's dataset in Kibana. Moreover, if you need to access data or start exploring anything, Kibana needs a data view. For example, a data view can point to one or more indices that have come up until now.

If you've added integration for new data, uploaded a file, or added sample data, data views will be created automatically by Kibana. However, if you are ingesting your own data, then we can perform the following steps to create a data view:

1. Go to the **Kibana** main menu and click on **Stack Management | Data views | Data Views under Kibana**. You should then see a screen like this:

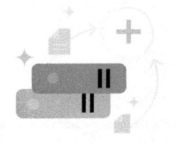

You have data in Elasticsearch. Now, create a data view.

Kibana requires a data view to identify which data streams, indices, and index aliases you want to explore. A data view can point to a specific index, for example, your log data from yesterday, or all indices that contain your log data.

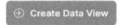

Want to learn more?   Read the docs ⍐

Figure 2.1 – The first step of creating a data view on Kibana

2. Once you click on **Create Data View**, it opens up a window to name the data view and add the **@timestamp** field of your dataset, which has date/timestamp information. The next screenshot shows this:

Figure 2.2 – The second step of creating a data view

3. Finally, we see the data view has been created, and you can see the fields present in the dataset along with the field mappings (data types) in the table, as listed in the following screenshot:

Figure 2.3 – The final step of data view creation

Once the data view is created, we can start using it in all the interfaces of Kibana, which will help you point to the collection of indices in the Elasticsearch cluster.

We have seen how data views can be created from scratch. Now, we will understand how spaces can help us start organizing our environment.

Creating spaces

Remember times when you had multiple people working together in the same UI environment and you struggled to properly organize individual work?

Spaces in Kibana will resolve that problem for you! Spaces allow us to organize objects into categories that you can define. Here are the steps to navigate and create a space:

1. Navigate to the main menu of Kibana, click on **Stack Management** | **Spaces**, *OR* click the green square box with **D** on it:

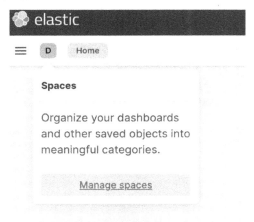

Figure 2.4 – Popup that opens when we click the Default button of spaces

Next, name the space, considering the audience that is going to use this environment. For example, we are creating a space for the Analyst team:

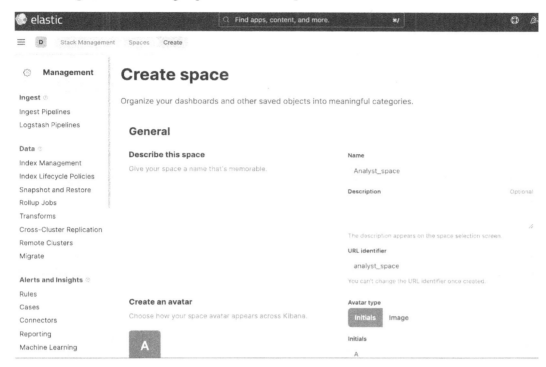

Figure 2.5 – Adding a name and URL identifier to the space creation proces2

2. If we scroll down on the same page, we can also find an option to edit the features available on Kibana for that particular space. Just to show an example of this, we have unchecked the **Dashboard** and **Canvas** features from the **Analytics** features for this space in the following screenshot. Then, click on **Create space**:

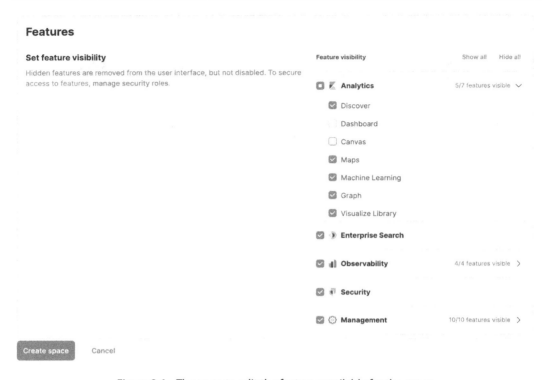

Figure 2.6 – The page to edit the features available for the space

3.   Once we create spaces as desired, we can view them in **Stack Management** or in the same dropdown from where we started! In the following screenshot, we have created an **Analyst** space and an **Engineer** space (following the same process).

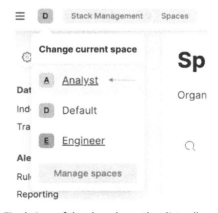

Figure 2.7– Final view of the dropdown that lists all spaces created

4. The final step is to switch on the newly created space by clicking the **Analyst** space from the preceding step and confirm whether it is exactly how we want the environment to be.

5. Also, when we log in next time to Kibana, we will see an option to select which space we wish to go in:

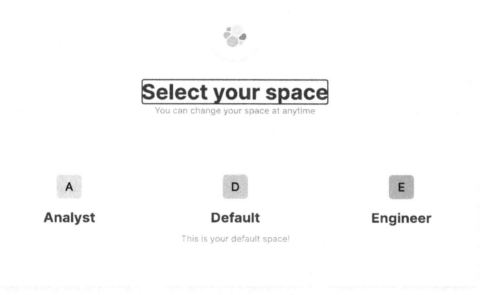

Figure 2.8 – The first page that opens when we log in to Kibana once we create spaces

In this section, we have understood the step-by-step process of how to create different spaces and level up the organization of our workspace. It comes in very handy for teams that have multiple people using the same instance of Elasticsearch and Kibana for their distinct goals.

Understanding saved objects in Kibana

Any object that we create on Kibana that includes an index pattern, a visualization, a canvas pad, or a dashboard is defined as a saved object. We can view, edit, export, and import these saved objects by going to the **Kibana** main menu and clicking on **Stack Management | Saved Objects**:

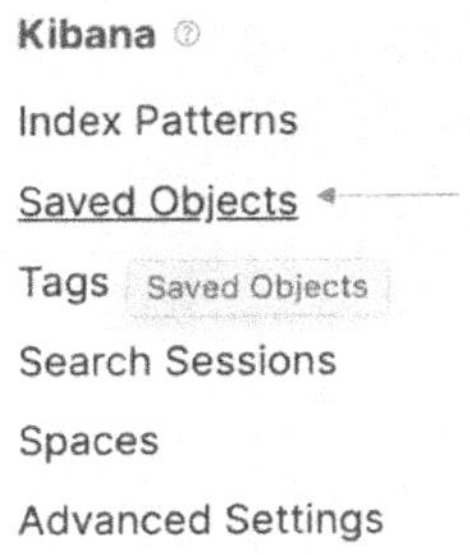

Kibana ⦾

Index Patterns

Saved Objects ◄------

Tags Saved Objects

Search Sessions

Spaces

Advanced Settings

Figure 2.9 – Dialog box with Saved Objects under Stack Management in the Kibana main menu

Import and **Export** are key functionalities that can help us to move objects across different Kibana instances or can be beneficial when we have different working environments.

Saved Objects also has a feature to share any of these saved objects across different spaces on Kibana, which will enable different users on your Kibana environment to be able to see/view/edit/delete these objects based on the permissions and authorizations we set. We will learn more about **role-based access control (RBAC)** in the upcoming chapters.

Summary

In this chapter, we took a deep dive into what data views are and explored the steps to create data views. This is an essential element to start working on various interfaces on Kibana and hence should not be skipped. We also studied the step-by-step process of creating spaces, thereby understanding how spaces help us to smartly organize our saved objects into specific categories. Saved objects, furthermore, enable us to perform various actions on things we create on Kibana.

In the next chapter, we will see how we can use the data views created in this lesson to start discovering and exploring our dataset in the **Discover** interface of Kibana.

3

Discovering the Data through Discover

So, you've got your data in. Now it's time to answer questions. What countries in the world have the maximum number of people working in IT? What events have the runtime error 404? Which customers are making the highest contribution to the profit?

All of these questions (and more!) can be discovered right on this interface. It is finally time to start exploring our dataset through the very interesting interface in Kibana, called **Discover**. Right when you start collecting and ingesting your data from your data sources, Discover in Kibana will be one place you would like to go and kickstart your exploration of the dataset. From which fields are coming in to how your data is structured with respect to the datatypes of the fields, everything can be visible in Discover. It also has an amazing query feature, which serves as your own custom search functionality placed over whatever dataset you have in the Elasticsearch cluster.

In this chapter, we shall take a deep dive into the main features as listed ahead, step by step, and explore all the different elements Discover provides us in order to leverage the search functionality to its optimum capacity:

- Exploring your data
- Working with queries
- Creating a saved search

Let's start data exploration and learn some key concepts about how data is stored and modeled in Elasticsearch to create a better understanding of the best use of Discover's search functionality.

Exploring your data

Let us now start looking into how the data gets stored in the Elasticsearch cluster, which takes us to the concept of a document. Anything that we ingest in the cluster gets stored in the cluster as a document.

Elasticsearch – a document store

Before starting to understand how exploration of data can be done, Elasticsearch is called a distributed document store as it stores the data in the form of serialized JSON documents:

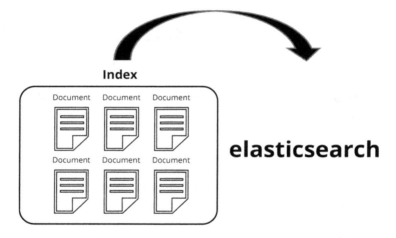

Figure 3.1 – An index with a collection of documents can be stored in Elasticsearch

These JSON documents are distributed across all the nodes of the cluster. If we go into where this document is stored in an index, it would be a logical namespace called an **Index**. It can be thought of as a collection of JSON documents that has data stored in the form of key-value pairs that contain the data. See the following example:

Sr. No	Name	Address	Visa status
1	John	United States	Approved

Figure 3.2 – A sample of a record of data

The preceding tabular structure of one record, if ingested into the Elasticsearch cluster, will be converted to a flat JSON document as follows:

```
{
"SrNo": 1,
"Name": "John",
```

```
"Address": "United States",
"VisaStatus": "Approved"
}
```

One field can be indexed in multiple ways for it to be searched for specific purposes. For example, a string field can be indexed as a text to use it for full-text search, and it can also be indexed as a keyword field to facilitate case-sensitive searching or sorting functionality, or to perform various aggregations on the data.

Let's talk more about the datatypes now.

Datatypes in Elasticsearch

It is very important to understand how your data is being modeled from the backend to use these datatypes, as it impacts the way the field is going to be searched.

The datatypes, typically called **field mappings** in Elasticsearch, will be dynamically assigned by default. **Date, IP, Text, Numeric, Boolean**, and **Geo points** are the key datatypes. Elasticsearch detects the datatypes and maps them to the respective field mapping. Hence, we can also call Elasticsearch schemaless, because we need not define the datatypes before the data gets ingested into the cluster.

In the Discover interface, in the left-most section, we can locate the available list of fields in the selected data view. The tiny icon beside each field denotes the type of field mapping each field is mapped to. This is shown in the following screenshot:

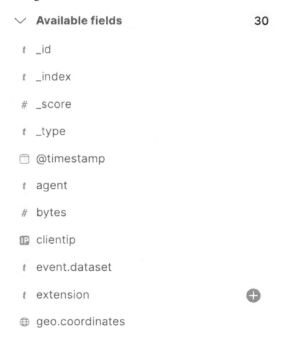

Figure 3.3 – The available fields list section on the Discover page of Kibana

The abbreviated icons can be understood as follows:

- **t**: String datatype
- **#**: Numeric datatype
- **Globe**: Geo point datatype
- **IP**: IP datatype
- **Calendar**: Date/timestamp datatype

As much as dynamic mappings work well for most cases, it is also a best practice to create your own mappings by creating an index first before ingesting the data so that you can model the fields as per the use case's search and write requirements.

Now that we have a good understanding of how a field is mapped to an appropriate datatype, let us start exploring the **Time filter** and **Data view** features in the Discover interface.

The Discover page

As we begin elaborating on the features of the Discover page, the two most important features to set the context of the search are described as follows:

- **Setting up a time filter**: This is one of the first steps we do when we visit the page for the first time. It is an essential step to perform that will show us the data in the range we set the time filter in. For example, by default, the time filter is set to previous 15 minutes, which means that Discover would be showing us the data that has come into the cluster in the previous 15 minutes. We can increase the time range or set up any particular date range in which we are looking to explore the data:

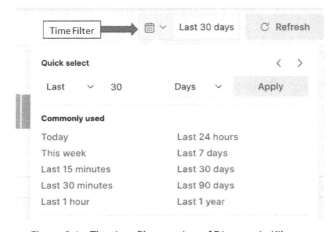

Figure 3.4 – The time filter section of Discover in Kibana

- **Selecting the data view**: Selecting which data view you wish to explore is a key step because that will determine which dataset you can now start exploring. You can select/switch between different data views through this drop-down feature. The following available list section will be updated dynamically as we select the type of data view:

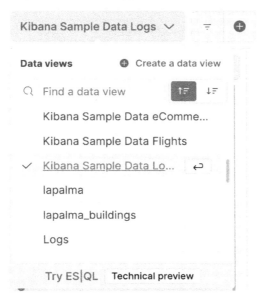

Figure 3.5 – The left-most section of Kibana to select the data view of Discover

So far, we have learned about a few initial features of the page, and now we'll move on to exploring the search part of the interface, which will enable us to perform certain search queries on our data in the cluster.

Working with queries

Imagine a world where a famous e-commerce website that you wish to shop from doesn't have a search bar! It is next to inevitable to have a feature to search, which in turn allows a user to type and do a quick look-up on the data. The constant need to search is increasing now, more than ever. In fact, every website, page, or frontend requires a search bar that facilitates the way a user can search the data:

Figure 3.6 – The Search bar

Let's start understanding the query language that is provided in the search bar of Discover.

Structuring KQL query (example)

Kibana Query Language, abbreviated as **KQL**, is a text-based query language that is used to filter data in Kibana. It works on a simple syntax of just searching for the terms we're looking for in the search bar, or being more specific on what we're searching for by providing a field against the word, shown as follows:

```
"field": "value"
```

For example, if I have a field called **Category** and I am searching for the term Engineering in that field, then I can frame my search as follows:

```
"Category": "engineering"
```

This will be a case-insensitive search as by default, it will access the text type of field mapping. It is important to note that, as we previously learned, our string fields are mapped twice – once as text field mapping and again as keyword field mapping. Hence, we can be specific here as to which field mapping we refer to for the search; for example, if we wish to do a case-sensitive search, we can do the following:

```
"Category.keyword":" Engineering"
```

The field parameter is optional, hence we can also perform the same search using just the term itself, which is as follows:

```
Engineering or engineering
```

The preceding search will search for the term across all the fields in the data view.

Pairing the queries with Boolean operators

We can combine different query criteria to search with the help of Boolean operators – and/or (case-insensitive). For example, if we have two fields to search on, category and error_code, then the search can be framed as follows:

```
"category": "engineering" AND "error_code": 404
```

Searching numeric fields

If we have numbers to work with, we could use operators such as >, <, >=, and <= and use them in different combinations of the Boolean operators, as stated in the preceding section. For example, if we want to have both types of operators implemented on two fields, category and bytes, then it can be done as follows:

```
"category": "engineering" OR "bytes" > 500
```

How to search when you don't know how to spell what you wish to search for

How many times have you googled an incorrect spelling of a word? There are numerous times when a user cannot spell the words correctly when searching. That is where the flexibility of having a typo comes into play, and we have the wildcard syntax to the rescue for the moment. For example, to find documents where `customer_firstname` starts with s, we can implement a KQL query as follows:

```
"customer_firstname": "s*"
```

Here, * matches to zero or more characters. If you want to only match one character, you can use the ? character.

In this section, we deep-dived into different ways to search your data across your cluster with the help of KQL. We also learned about distinct features to add flexibility to search the data in case users are unaware of the exact terms they are searching for. If we wish to leverage the Lucene query language in place of a filter, we can switch to Lucene from KQL by clicking the **Query menu** icon, as shown in the following screenshot:

Figure 3.7 – The Query menu option in Discover

Once we've navigated inside this menu, we can click **language:KQL** to select the **Lucene** option available there, as shown in the following screenshot:

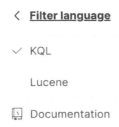

Figure 3.8 – The navigation to select KQL/Lucene

Let's level this up by understanding the concept of filters in Discover, which do the same job but with better ease of access and use.

Understanding filters

Queries such as KQL help us to create search statements based on specific criteria, but we can also use filters as sticky queries that help us to create pretty much the exact same results as queries, but with more flexibility to perform various actions such as negate, pin, disable, and delete. Refer to the following screenshot:

Figure 3.9 – Navigating to the place from where you can add filters

The process of creating a filter is straightforward, where you select a field from the drop-down menu and enter the values it needs to match to form a search:

Figure 3.10 – The step-by-step process to creating a filter on Kibana

The moment we create a filter or a KQL query, it is going to convert to a **domain-specific language** query in the backend, which is going to interact with Elasticsearch and get the response back to us in the space called **document table**. There will be a list of documents, which, if expanded (by clicking the **Expand** button, as shown in *Figure 3.10*), will show us the data in tabular format as well as the JSON format:

Figure 3.11 – Using the Expand button to view detailed documents in Discover

Have a look at the following screenshot to view the expanded document:

Expanded document

View: ☐ Single document   ☒ Surrounding documents ⑦ |< < 1 of **500** >

| Table | **JSON** |

🔍 Search field names

Actions	Field	Value
_k_	_id	rEsXdYwBvvfAn5mwbNZX
_k_	_index	.ds-kibana_sample_data_logs-2023.12.17-000001
_#_	_score	-
🗓	@timestamp	Dec 23, 2023 @ 08:15:19.548
_t_	agent	Mozilla/5.0 (X11; Linux i686) AppleWebKit/534.24 (KHTML, like Gecko) hrome/11.0.696.50 Safari/534.24
_#_	bytes	7,443
_#_	bytes_counter	17,058,178
_#_	bytes_gauge	7,443

Figure 3.12 – The expanded view of the JSON document on the document table in Discover, Kibana

Furthermore, to give you some more insight into the trend/flow of the data in the cluster, Discover has a very interesting graph on the top, which is called a data histogram:

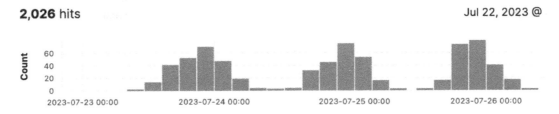

Figure 3.13 – The data histogram visualization/graph made by Kibana on Discover

In this section, we took a deep dive into understanding how various different features of the Discover interface work and how you can leverage all of these functionalities to kickstart exploring the data present in your cluster.

In the next section, we will learn how to save a search in order to start utilizing it in your dashboards.

Creating a saved search

A saved search is a search created by saving the search results of the query done by KQL or a filter on Discover. It can be further used to add in as a saved search on a dashboard to display a specific set of documents representing a specific use case/query.

A saved search can also be a great way to reuse the search made on Discover. Furthermore, the results in the form of documents can be added to the dashboard along with the other visualizations. Let us see how we can create a saved search, step by step.

Steps to create a saved search

Creating a saved search is a fairly simple process where you have a specific use case in mind and need to host your search in that exact direction. Let's see how to begin with creating a saved search:

1. Go to the main menu of Kibana and open **Discover**:

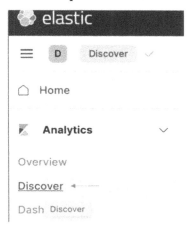

Figure 3.14 – The navigation of the main menu and Discover

2. Select the data view according to the dataset you wish to work on:

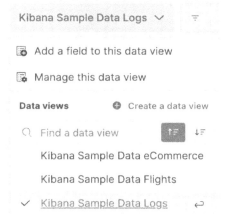

Figure 3.15 – Selecting the data view on Discover, Kibana

3. Select the use-case-appropriate date range in the time filter:

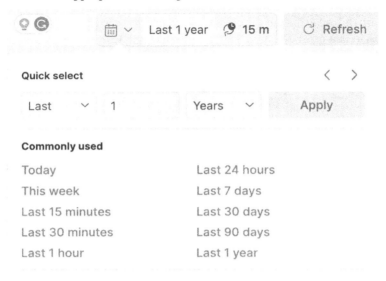

Figure 3.16 – Selecting the time filter on Discover, Kibana

4. Implement a search in the form of KQL, a filter, or both:

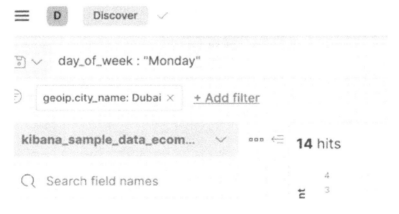

Figure 3.17 – Implementing the KQL query and filter on Discover, Kibana

5.   Go to the **Save** option in the top-right corner and save it with a relevant name:

14 hits

> Aug 15, 2023 @ 09:58:34.000

Time ↓   **Document**

> Aug 15, 2023 @ 09:58:34.000   day_of_week: **Monday** geoip.city_name: **Dubai** category: Men's Clothin
                                   email: robbie@moran-family.zzz event.dataset: sample_ecommerce geo
                                   order_date: Aug 15, 2023 @ 09:58:34.000 order_id: 566671 products.
                                   products.created_on: Dec 13, 2016 @ 10:58:34.000, Dec 13, 2016 @ 10
                                   products.price: $50.00, $37.00 products.product_id: 22,991, 17,752

> Aug 15, 2023 @ 05:55:12.000   day_of_week: **Monday** geoip.city_name: **Dubai** category: Women's Shoes
                                   (empty) day_of_week_i: 0 email: mary@davidson-family.zzz event.dat
                                   manufacturer: Pyramidustries, Gnomehouse order_date: Aug 15, 2023 @
                                   products.category: Women's Shoes, Women's Clothing products.created
                                   products.min_price: $15.07, $24.02 products.price: $28.98, $50.00

> Aug 15, 2023 @ 05:09:07.000   day_of_week: **Monday** geoip.city_name: **Dubai** category: Women's Cloth
                                   (empty) day_of_week_i: 0 email: rabbia al@wise-family.zzz event.da
                                   manufacturer: Champion Arts, Oceanavigations order_date: Aug 15, 20
                                   products.category: Women's Clothing, Women's Shoes products.created
                                   products.min_price: $9.68, $33.78 products.price: $18.98, $65.00 p

Figure 3.18 – The document table showing the highlighted
terms found, once searched on Discover, Kibana

Once we create the search and receive the results in the documents table, we can then navigate to saving it by clicking the **Save** button at the top of the page:

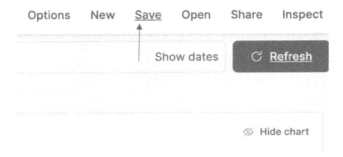

Figure 3.19 – Navigating to Save on Discover, Kibana

This will navigate you to a dialog box with an option to write a name for the saved search (as shown in *Figure 3.19*). Then, finally, click **Save** for it to get saved in the library:

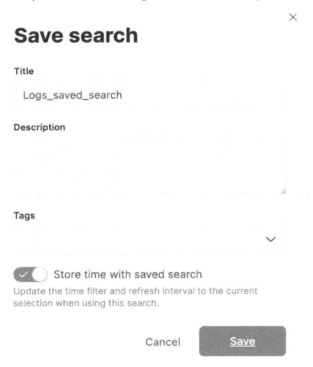

Figure 3.20 – Navigating to name the saved search and clicking Save on Discover, Kibana

In this section on creating a saved search, we learned the granular steps of deriving a search result out of the KQL and filters that we studied in the previous part. A saved search is a great and convenient way of displaying documents in the dashboard as a part of your insights summary in order to generate conclusions from the data.

Summary

In this chapter, we studied how to explore different search features to create a query language syntax that can filter our data and show us the results in Discover. We can play around with this UI to leverage the features as needed.

Next up, we shall explore how we can draw distinct types of visualizations in Kibana based on the data in an Elasticsearch cluster.

Part 2: Visualizations in Kibana

In this part, we will unlock the power of **Time Series Visual Builder** (**TSVB**) and Lens visualizations as your gateways to near real-time insights. You will see how to replace static dashboards with near real-time updates at lightning speed to capture every fleeting trend and nuance with TSVB. Moreover, you'll craft intricate time series magic, while Lens transforms your data into mesmerizing maps and geospatial stories.

This part has the following chapters:

- *Chapter 4, How about We Visualize?*
- *Chapter 5, Powering Visualizations with Near Real-Time Updates*

4

How About We Visualize?

The best way to clearly understand what your data is all about is to visualize it. And everyone appreciates a visually stunning Kibana dashboard, with its assortment of graphs and representations that display real-time data. From simple pie charts or vertical bar graphs to interactive map visualizations, the ability to manipulate and analyze data is what Kibana excels at. But before you can enjoy the beauty of a well-designed Kibana dashboard, several essential milestones must be taken.

While experienced Kibana users may breeze through these steps effortlessly, for most users, they can prove to be quite challenging. It requires both experience and a deep understanding of your dataset and the features such as the Visualize library in Kibana. This chapter aims to assist those who are struggling with their initial attempts at visualizing data in Kibana. It is time to learn to effectively visualize data using this powerful functionality of creating a specific graph designed to serve a purpose. In this chapter, we will start exploring the visualization functionality in detail.

The following are the topics covered in this chapter:

- Exploring Lens visualizations
- Deep diving into the backend of visualizations on Kibana
- Understanding Canvas, Maps, and Markdown visualizations

Technical requirements

As per the basic requirement, we assume that you have data ingested in the cluster and that Kibana is set up on the nodes of (any) environment (cloud or local).

Once Kibana is up and running, we can navigate to **Kibana** home page and click on **Try sample data | Other sample datasets**, then click on **Add data for Kibana_sample_data_ecommerce dataset**.

We will be using this dataset for creating a visualization on Lens in this chapter.

Exploring Lens visualizations

If you're a newbie in the field of visualizing data, then you have come to the right place! If you are not sure how you wish to get started on creating a visualization or which type of visualization you wish to use to represent your data, Lens is a great way to simply drag and drop the fields you want to build a graph on. And voilà – it will create a vertical bar graph to start with. We can change the type of the graph to any other representation that we prefer later.

The ease and flexibility of the drag-and-drop experience is what makes the Lens visualization one sure spot for pretty much everything that one wishes to do with representing data in the form of a visualization.

Let us look at the process of creating a sample Lens visualization process step by step:

1. Get to know the **Lens** page; there is a name for everything on the interface, as shown in the following screenshot:

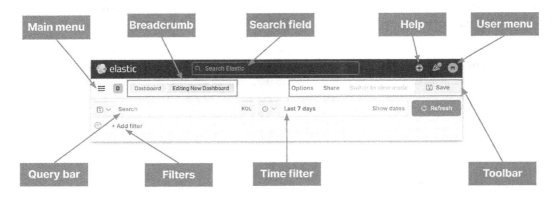

Figure 4.1 – Layout of the Lens interface in Kibana

2. Go to the main menu of Kibana and select **Visualize Library**:

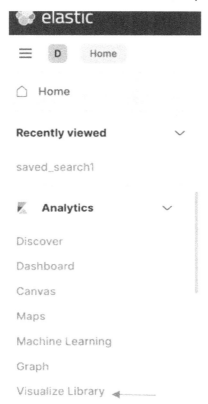

Figure 4.2 – Navigating to the Visualize library in Kibana

3. Click on the **Create visualization** button in the top right-hand corner of the page:

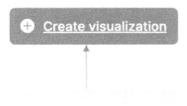

Figure 4.3 – Create visualization button in Kibana

4.   Then, select the **Lens** option from all the options available on the interface:

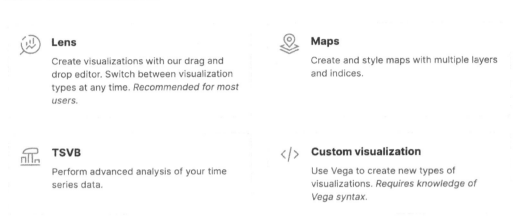

Figure 4.4 – Selecting a Lens visualization in Kibana

5.   This is what the interface of Lens looks like! We start by selecting **Data view** (in this case, we select **kibana_sample_data_ecommerce** under the dropdown):

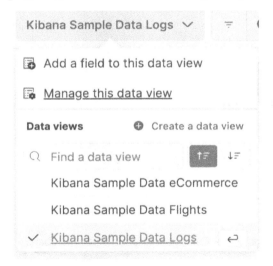

Figure 4.5 – The selection dropdown for Data view in Kibana

Let's also select a time filter according to the time range for which we wish to represent the data. It can be minutes, hours, days, weeks, months, or years, or we can also select a specific date (from and to) in the filter:

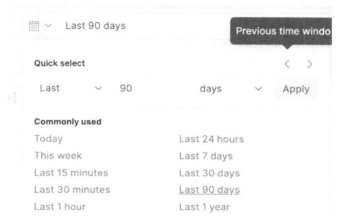

Figure 4.6 – Time filter in Kibana Lens

6.   Begin with dragging and dropping a field (for example, the **category.Keyword** field from the **Kibana_sample_data_ecommerce** dataset). It will automatically assign the field on the horizontal axis while your vertical axis will take the metric field, which is by default the count field. We can create a visualization, as shown here:

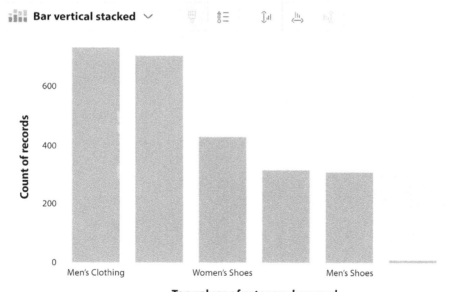

Figure 4.7 – Vertical bar graph created by dragging and dropping
the category.keyword field in the workspace

7.   We can also change to other types of visualization by clicking the dropdown shown ahead. This will give a good option to switch between different types of graphs in just one interface:

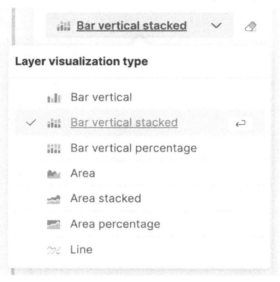

Figure 4.8 – Window that opens after we click the Chart type dropdown on a Lens visualization

For example, if we select a pie chart under the dropdown, it will switch the view from a vertical bar graph to a pie chart, as seen here:

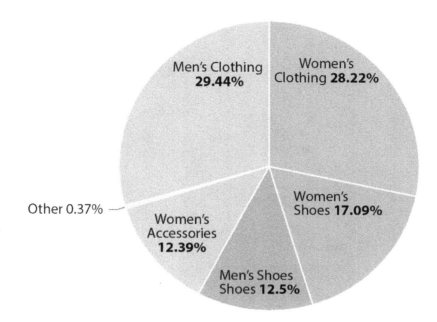

Figure 4.9 – Pie chart created on a Lens visualization

Now, switch back to the vertical bar graph to explore more things on the interface.

If we see the layer pane on the right-hand side of the interface, it will have fields assigned to the horizontal axis and vertical axis according to the fields we dragged and dropped onto the workspace.

The **Horizontal axis** setting will look like this:

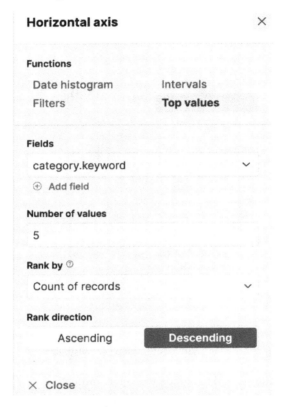

Figure 4.10 – Window that opens after we click the Horizontal axis
setting on the layer pane on a Lens visualization

We can edit the values here as per the requirements. The sorting order of the buckets on the visualization can be ranked as per the **Rank direction** option selected on the **Horizontal axis** setting on the layer pane.

8. If we click the **Vertical axis** setting on the layer pane, it will look like the following:

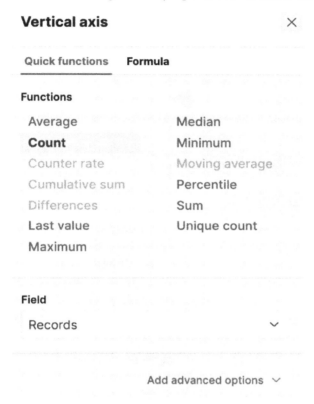

Figure 4.11– Window that opens after we click the Vertical axis
setting on the layer pane on a Lens visualization

Quick functions are basic aggregations that Elasticsearch provides us to be done on the vertical axis. Depending on the data type of the field selected, the functions will be enabled/disabled.

9. Once we are done with the changes we want, we can navigate to the top-right corner and click **Save**:

Inspect
Download as CSV
Save
Refresh

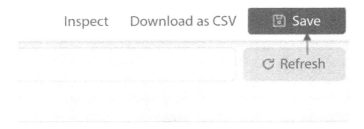

Figure 4.12 – Save button on a Lens visualization in Kibana

This will let us name this visualization, save it to the Visualize library, and/or quickly add it to a new or existing dashboard of your choosing:

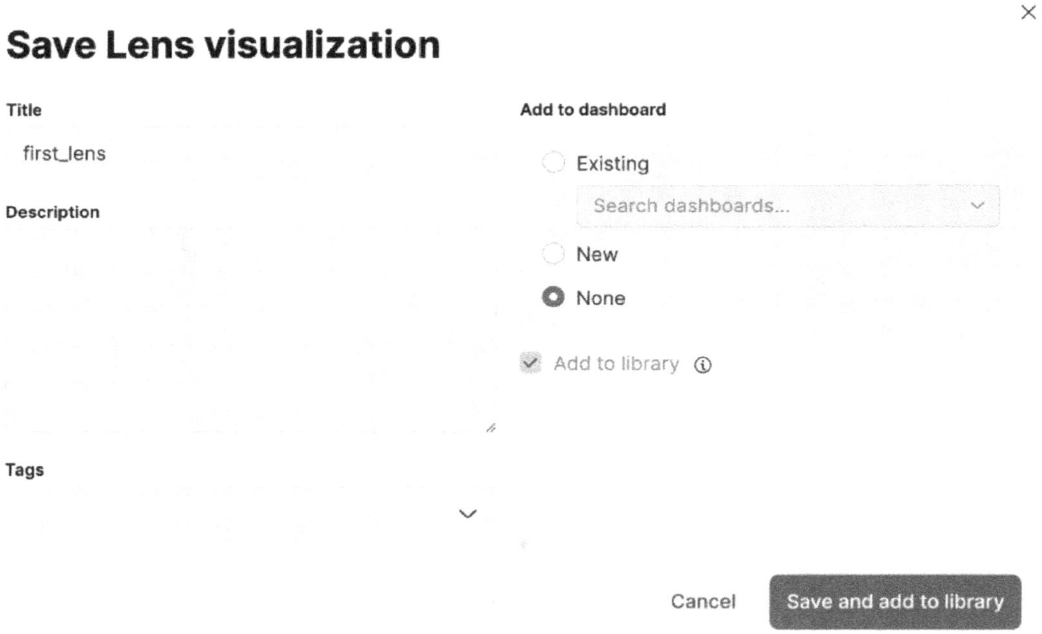
Save Lens visualization
Title
first_lens
Description
Tags
Add to dashboard
Existing
Search dashboards...
New
None
Add to library
Cancel
Save and add to library

Figure 4.13 – Naming a Lens visualization in Kibana

In this section, we learned the key process to build a lens visualization. Now, let us take a look at what drives these visualizations on the frontend. We will begin by understanding the process that happens under the hood in the next section.

Deep diving into the backend of visualizations in Kibana

A visualization is simple to understand and create because, as we all know, it is on the frontend. But what powers up this visualization on Kibana from the backend is your aggregations. Elasticsearch aggregations help us to analyze our data with metrics or statistics, which require certain calculations to be done in the backend. So, you may have questions in your use case:

- Who are the most popular customers in my e-commerce dataset?

- What category of sales made the most profit in my business?

- What is the minimum runtime per day for my log data?

- What is the unique number of countries that are contributing to my geographical data?

All these questions can be answered by implementing various aggregations on Elasticsearch. The aggregations can be divided into key categories:

- **Metric aggregations**: Any problem statement that requires Elasticsearch to perform analytics as a mathematical formula on numeric fields can be resolved by implementing metric aggregations. Metric visualizations in Kibana will make this work easier for us as it provides us with the Kibana Visualize library as a UI interface to do the same.

  For example, if we create a visualization on metrics, it is called **metric visualization**. The steps to do the same will be very similar to how we created the output in *Figure 4.7* earlier, except this time, we will select a numeric field to drag and drop into the workspace to create a metric type of visualization. Once created, it will be displayed on Lens Kibana as follows:

$$\$64.74$$
Median of taxful_total_price

Figure 4.14 – An example of a metric visualization done on the total_
price field from the sample dataset on Kibana Lens

- **Bucket aggregations**: Whenever there is a need to group your data into categories called **buckets** based on a certain common criterion that the document follows, we use bucket aggregations for those use-case scenarios; for example, grouping data into buckets based on a field value, a time range, or any such criteria in the dataset. Visualizations on Kibana such as *terms*, *histograms*, *data_histograms*, *ranges*, and so on are based on these bucket aggregations.

  For example, if we perform a terms (bucket) aggregation to find out the top values of product manufacturers in an e-commerce dataset, then it will create top values of the buckets, and documents in each bucket will share the same criteria; in this case, it is the same manufacturer. If it is replicated on the visualization on Kibana Lens, it can be displayed as follows:

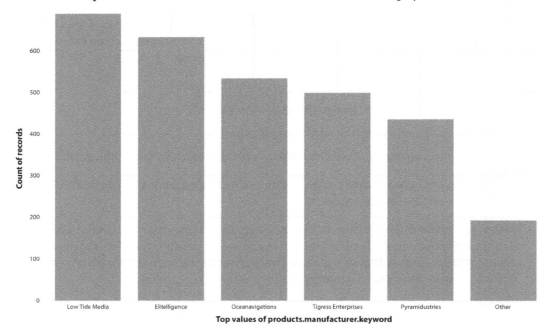

Figure 4.15 – An example of a vertical bar graph that is working on a bucket aggregation called terms aggregation done on the products.manufacturer.keyword field on Kibana Lens

In this section, we understood the concepts responsible for deriving visualization results on the Kibana UI. It is time to explore other kinds of visualizations on Kibana that can be done through the Kibana main menu, so let's get started.

Understanding Canvas, Maps, and Markdown visualizations

We have seen visualizations where we had a definitive purpose in mind with respect to what we'd like to do with the analysis. However, when we have intricately custom use cases such as adding our own images to highlight our company/customer information, we would need to create a **Canvas** visualization. A Canvas visualization is very similar to a literal white canvas that makes you, the artist, create/draw/add anything you like and make it interesting to present.

If you need to look at data points coming from different parts of the world, then we might need a map, which lets us create a visualization on a world map to display data in the form of different symbols. To add anything to the dashboard that is related to text, Markdown is a great visualization to start with. Let's start looking at each one of them step by step.

Building Canvas visualizations

Canvas is a powerful tool for visualizing and presenting data. It allows users to extract real-time information from Elasticsearch and combine it with various elements such as colors, pictures, and text to create dynamic and visually appealing representations. Whether you are creatively inclined or technically savvy, Canvas offers endless possibilities. We can fully customize our workspace by adding background colors, changing different types of fonts, and making it interesting to look at. We have numerous options to add elements on a white plane screen called a workpad. We can also personalize this workpad by incorporating our own visualizations that we create in Kibana. It connects with the backend seamlessly and helps us showcase it through different workpad elements that come in the form of different shapes, charts, and monitors that are unique to Canvas. For example, for the following workpad, we can see many different elements being added in the form of different shapes, colors, text, and visualizations:

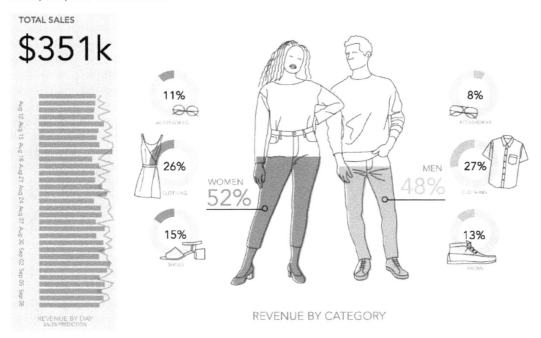

Figure 4.16 – Canvas workpad created from the sample e-commerce dataset

Let us look at the step-by-step process to create a Canvas workpad:

1. Go to the Kibana main menu and click on **Canvas**:

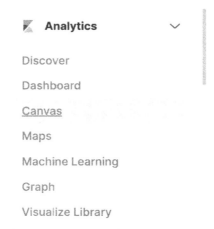

Figure 4.17 – Navigating to the Canvas tool in the main menu

2. Once we go to **Canvas**, we click **Create a workpad**. A visualization created on Canvas will be called a workpad:

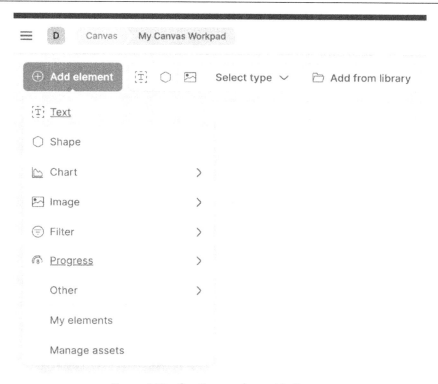

Figure 4.18 – Creating an element in Canvas

When we click the **Add element** button in the top-left corner of the screen, it lets us choose how we wish to start creating the workpad. We can add texts through the Markdown syntax (we will talk more about this in the upcoming topic), create shapes, add different kinds of charts that are not found on other visualizations, add images from the local device, monitor progress charts, and so on.

For example, let's say we selected a **Chart** type of element and added a bubble chart:

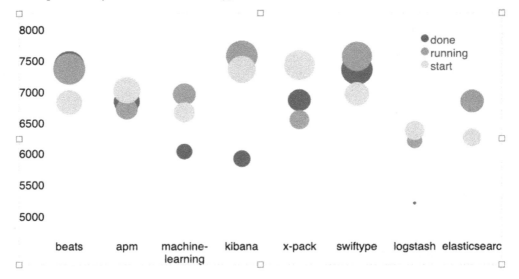

Figure 4.19 – An example element of Canvas

If we click the bubble chart and go to the pane on the right-hand side, it will give us four different options to choose how to connect the data to the charts we have chosen on the workpad, as shown here:

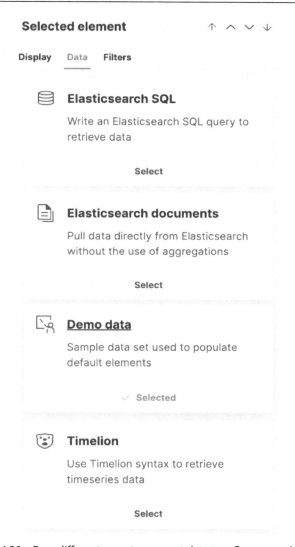

Figure 4.20 – Four different ways to connect data to a Canvas workpad

By default, it will have **Demo data** selected, but we can change it to anything else. Once done, we can start sharing it by generating a PDF report out of it through the **Share** button on the top, or we can also download that as a JSON file on the local system.

Canvas provides an intuitive platform for creating captivating presentations that effectively convey complex data in a visually compelling manner. The combination of live data integration, rich infographics, and filtering capabilities makes Canvas an invaluable tool for anyone looking to transform raw information into meaningful insights.

Building Maps visualizations

You can transform your geographical data into stunning maps with our innovative Maps tool in Kibana. Maps allows us to create geographic maps that are not only visually appealing but also highly insightful. Let's start building a Maps visualization and check the process as follows:

1. Navigate to the Kibana main menu, then go to **Maps**:

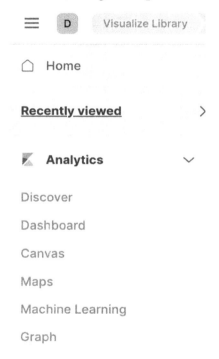

Figure 4.21 – Navigating to Maps in Kibana

2. Once we click on **Maps**, it takes us to the Maps interface, which typically displays a world map. We begin by setting up a use-case-appropriate time filter, and then navigate to the **Add layers** button on the right-hand side of the Maps interface:

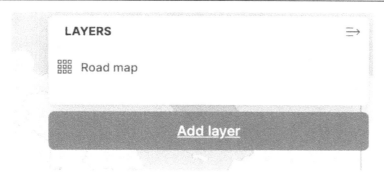

Figure 4.22 – Navigating to Add layer

3. Click on **Add layer**. The next page will show the many different ways to start adding layers to Maps visualizations. A layer is simply a way to connect your data to Maps visualizations.

It is essential to have a geopoint field present/mapped in your dataset that has latitude and longitude coordinates in order to create a Maps graph. You will be using the `flights` dataset here. You can follow the path of **Kibana** home page and clicking on **Try sample data | Other Sample datasets**, then click on **Add data for sample flight data**.

Next, coming back to **Maps**, on the **Add layer** page, let's say we select the **Documents** layer:

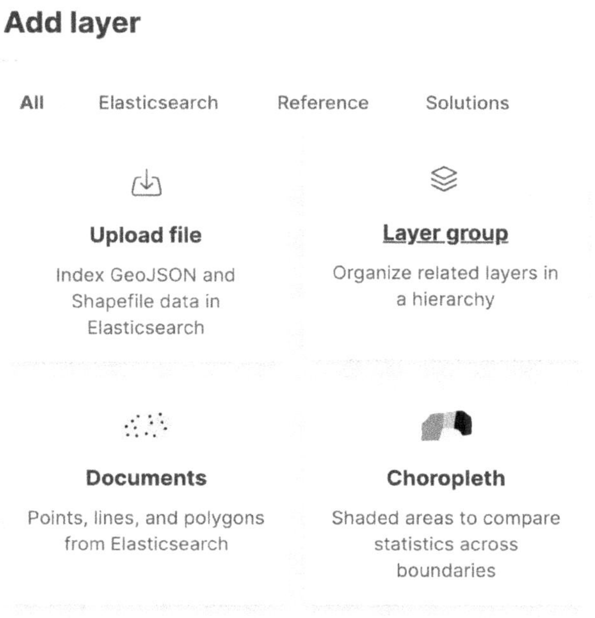

Add layer

All   Elasticsearch   Reference   Solutions

Upload file

Index GeoJSON and Shapefile data in Elasticsearch

Layer group

Organize related layers in a hierarchy

Documents

Points, lines, and polygons from Elasticsearch

Choropleth

Shaded areas to compare statistics across boundaries

Figure 4.23 – Four of the many ways to add layers to maps

4. Inside the **Documents** layer, select a **Data view/Index pattern** type you wish to work on and a **Geospatial field** type, then click on **Add layer** at the bottom:

Figure 4.24 – The page to select an index pattern and geospatial field

The result should display many tiny green dots on the Maps visualization, which will represent the destination location of the flights on the graph in this case, which looks like the following:

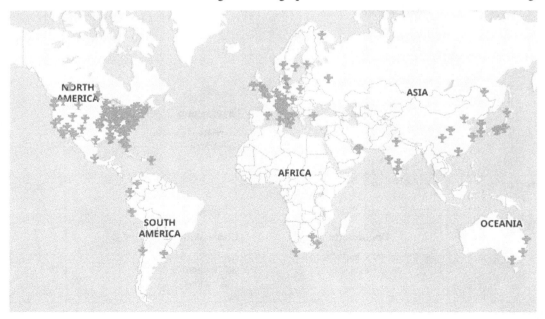

Figure 4.25 – The result of the Documents layer

5. Many formatting options can be applied on this layer, such as adjusting the opacity of the color of icons, zoom levels, fill/border color, size, orientation, and so on. One of the features also includes changing dots to icons and is called **airfield**, as displayed here:

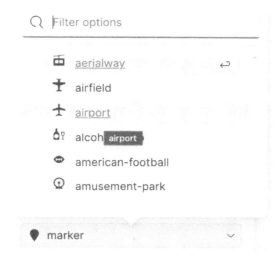

Figure 4.26 – Formatting options in the Documents layer

In this way, you can leverage different layers on the visualization and create a representation suitable to the use case; however, it is essential to ensure we are making the graph as clear and as easy to understand as possible. Too much overlap of shapes/colors could serve as one of the reasons users might not be able to decipher what you are communicating through the visualization.

For example, the following graph shows distinct layers to create different colors yet easy-to-read things:

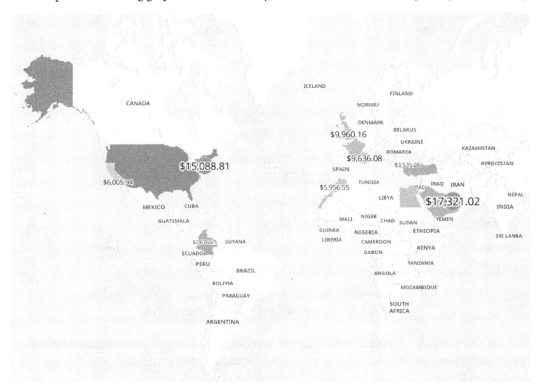

Figure 4.27 – The result of creating many such layers in Maps

In this section, we studied in detail how a Maps visualization can be created and used to display data coming from different parts of the world on a single screen in Kibana. Let's now explore a very different yet very useful visualization – a Markdown visualization – in the next section.

Building Markdown visualizations

Okay – so, you now know how to create visualizations. But how do we let a new user know what exactly these visualizations on a dashboard are all about? We use Markdown.

Markdown is the simplest way to add text to your dashboard. For any information, explanation, or a link for the audience to redirect themselves to the next dashboard (for example), Markdown is one sure solution to it all. It has a GitHub-flavored convention and CSS syntax that is straightforward to understand and implement. Let's see the steps to create a Markdown visualization:

1. Navigate to the main menu and find the **Visualize** library, then select a square that has T written on it, as shown in the following screenshot:

New visualization

                                                                     ✕

 Lens

Create visualizations with our drag and drop editor. Switch between visualization types at any time. *Recommended for most users.*

 Maps

Create and style maps with multiple layers and indices.

 TSVB

Perform advanced analysis of your time series data.

 Custom visualization

Use Vega to create new types of visualizations. *Requires knowledge of Vega syntax.*

 Aggregation based

Use our classic visualize library to create charts based on aggregations.

Explore options →

Tools

Text
Add text and images to your dashboard.
Input controls   **Deprecated**
Input controls are deprecated and will be removed in a future version.

Want to learn more?   Read documentation

Figure 4.28 – The navigational first step to Markdown

2. We can now start following the Markdown convention syntax to write text as needed. The following is one example where we are writing text as well as adding a hyperlink for the next dashboard:

Figure 4.29 – An example of Markdown

That's it. We can save this visualization by clicking on the **Save** button at the top and start using it to add to dashboards. (We will explore what dashboards are in the upcoming chapters.)

In this section, we studied the concept of Markdown in detail and understood the step-by-step process with an example. We can add not only text but also paragraphs, bullet points, links, and images to this Markdown visualization, which gives our dashboards an extra nudge to clearly explain what we try to display through the visual representations of our datasets. And the story doesn't end here. We can club all of these pieces of puzzles into one page and create a dashboard. It could look similar to this:

Figure 4.30 – An example of a dashboard

Let us dig into this in the upcoming chapters soon.

Summary

In this chapter, we explored and deep-dived into how different types of visualizations can be created and saved to a library or added to a dashboard. We explored a Lens visualization as one sure solution to many problems, with the help of two types of aggregations: metric and bucket aggregations, which work for us in the backend to retrieve the data. We also studied how geospatial fields that have geographical coordinates mapped to them in the data can be used to create a Maps visualization to pictorially display data on a world map. Also, we saw that Canvas, on the other hand, helps us create every type of view that could be part of a completely custom-defined requirement for a use case.

In the upcoming chapter, we will see how we utilize these visualizations to create a view called a dashboard that will help us connect a lot of dots in establishing important relationships within our data in the cluster.

5
Powering Visualizations with Near Real-Time Updates

Time Series Visual Builder (**TSVB**) is a powerful tool that allows you to create and display a wide range of visualizations on dashboards. With TSVB, you have the flexibility to combine an infinite number of aggregations to effectively display and analyze your data.

One of the key features of TSVB is its ability to annotate time series data with specific attention to timestamped events from an Elasticsearch index. This allows you to easily correlate events with certain points in your data and gain deeper insights. In addition to this, TSVB offers various types of visualizations such as data tables, charts, and Markdown panels, enabling you to choose the most suitable format for presenting your data. Furthermore, TSVB allows you to display multiple data views within each visualization, allowing for comprehensive analysis and comparison. The tool also provides custom functions and math capabilities on aggregations, giving you greater control over how your data is manipulated and presented. Finally, TSVB provides options for customization, such as adding colors and text, to further enhance the clarity and understanding of your visualizations.

Let's understand TSVB step by step with the following topics:

* Understanding TSVB
* Exploring the Metric, Top N, Gauge, Markdown, and Table types of TSVB visualizations
* Using Annotations

Technical requirements

For the basic requirements, we assume that you have data ingested in the cluster and that Elasticsearch and Kibana are set up on the nodes of any environment (cloud or local).

Once Kibana is up and running, navigate to **Kibana | Try sample data**, select **Other sample datasets**, and click on the **Add data for Kibana_sample_data_ecommerce** dataset.

We shall be using this dataset for creating the visualization on Lens in this chapter.

Understanding how to create TSVB visualizations

To get started with TSVB, simply open the tool and customize the necessary settings. With TSVB, you have the flexibility to create visualizations using only data views or Elasticsearch index strings. When utilizing data views, you gain the ability to create visualizations with runtime fields, incorporate URL drilldowns, add interactive filters for time series visualizations, and ultimately, enhance performance.

The path to navigate to TSVB is the **Kibana** homepage | **Visualize library** | **New visualization** | **TSVB**.

The screen should look like this:

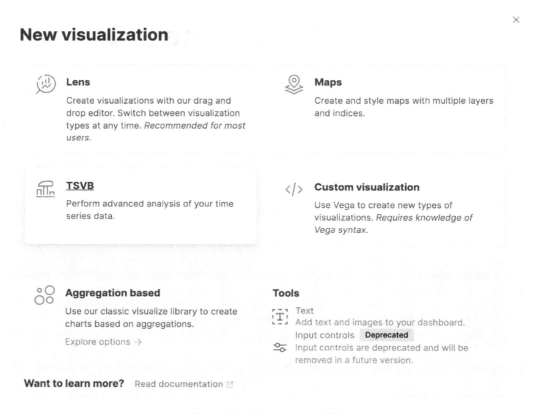

Figure 5.1 – Navigating to TSVB

TSVB provides users with the ability to create multiple series, which essentially act as separate Elasticsearch aggregations. Users can utilize the **Options** tab, as shown in the following figure:

Figure 5.2 – The Options tab in TSVB

Here, users can control the styling and formatting options for each series, with these options being inherited from **Panel options**. This allows for the easy comparison of different Elasticsearch indices and the ability to view two distinct time ranges from the same index.

When going to TSVB, the first page we land on is the **Time Series** page, which lets us select a data view in the **Panel options** tab, as shown in the following screenshot:

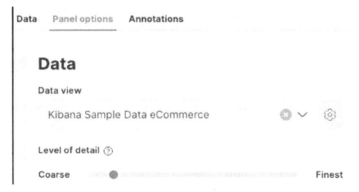

Figure 5.3 – The selection of Data view in TSVB

So far, we have understood how TSVB is accessed through the **Visualize library** tab in the **Kibana** main menu.

Now, let's get into how we can connect this graph to the data in the Elasticsearch cluster and use TSVB to drive near real-time insights from the data by understanding the **Aggregation** dropdown in the **Data** tab.

Understanding the Aggregation dropdown in the Data tab

In the **Data** tab, we can navigate to an **Aggregation** dropdown that lets us select what type of analysis we need to do on the dataset. There are various types of aggregations that we can implement, as shown in the following screenshot:

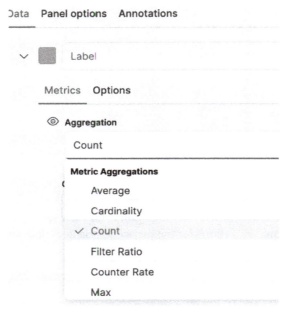

Figure 5.4 – The Aggregation dropdown

Filter Ratio, **Counter Rate**, **Positive Only**, **Series Agg**, and **Math** are some very frequently used functions to analyze the data. Let us understand each of these here:

- **Filter Ratio**: In TSVB, this allows you to analyze the error rate of events over time. By comparing two sets of documents, this metric provides a percentage value that highlights the proportion of errors in relation to the overall events. This insightful calculation helps to identify patterns and trends in data, enabling informed decision-making for optimizing performance and minimizing errors. A very good example of **Filter Ratio** is the use case where you wish to compare the ratio of the data with respect to two different cities. For example, for the `kibana_sample_dataset_ecommerce` sample dataset, if we are comparing data from two cities by creating a **KQL** (short for **Kibana Query Language**) query such as `geoip.city_name: "Cannes"` and `geoip.city_name: "Monte Carlo"`, we can add the implementation and create the visualization as follows:

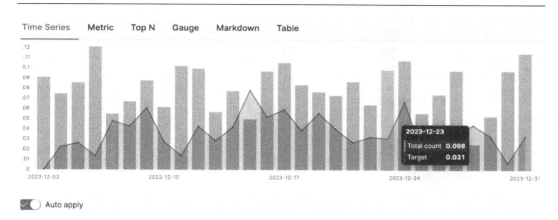

Figure 5.5 – The example for Filter Ratio

Here, we can create two different time series by clicking the + icon (shown in *Figure 5.20*) on the extreme right-hand side of the time series and changing the color to a different one, which will help us to distinguish between the two graphs created. We can select the **Filter Ratio** aggregation in the **Aggregation** dropdown and add the two KQL queries that we mentioned earlier in the **Numerator** part of the time series. The implementation to create the preceding graph can be configured as shown in the following screenshot:

Figure 5.6 – The example of aggregation configuration for Filter Ratio

We can change the representation style of the graph on the top by going to the **Options** tab and selecting a different type under the **Chart type** option, as shown in the following screenshot:

Figure 5.7 – Navigating to change the graph representation style

On the same page, you can leverage **Filter** by using KQL queries to essentially filter out documents based on a certain specific scenario. The **Fill (0 to 1)** option helps you create a graph with a darker or lighter shade of color in the TSVB visualization.

- **Counter Rate**: This is a useful tool when working with counters that consistently increase over time. It provides a convenient shortcut for calculating the maximum value, taking the derivative, and considering only positive values. By using **Counter Rate**, you can easily analyze and track the rate at which your counters are increasing, allowing you to gain valuable insights into your data trends and patterns. For example, if we implement the **Counter Rate** aggregation on `product.base_unit_price` in the same dataset, it gives us a graph as shown in the following screenshot:

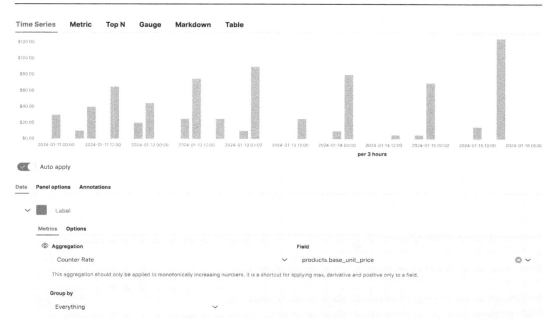

Figure 5.8 – The example for Counter Rate

- **Positive Only**: By using **Positive Only**, TSVB effectively eliminates any negative values from the results, making it a valuable tool for postprocessing data after a derivative calculation. By removing these negative values, analysts can focus solely on the positive aspects of the data, leading to more accurate and insightful analysis.

- **Series Agg**: This feature in TSVB applies a function to each individual series within a group. It then reduces the values of each series to a single number, which is represented as a single Y value per X value.

- **Math**: TSVB provides a range of math functions to perform mathematical calculations on each series of data. However, it is recommended to use **Math** only for the final function in each series.

- **Pipeline types of aggregations**: These are the aggregations that can be created by adding two types of metrics in the same time series in TSVB by clicking the + icon under the **Metrics** tab of the series. It can be implemented as follows:

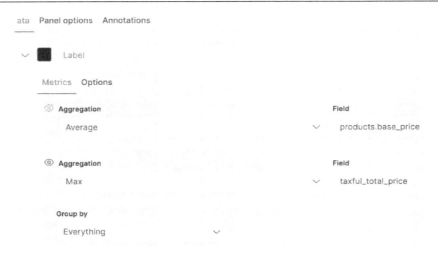

Figure 5.9 – The example for pipeline aggregation

Here, in the example, we are first calculating the average of the `products.base_price` field in the sample e-commerce dataset and then taking the output of this aggregation as an input to the second aggregation. For the second, we are calculating the maximum of `taxful_total_price`, which builds a graph like the following:

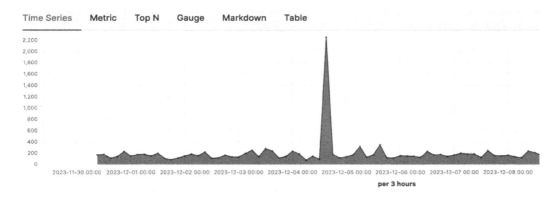

Figure 5.10 – The visualization created for pipeline aggregation

This figure significantly depicts the point where the peak happens, which is also the point where the calculated price is at the maximum.

With this, we have understood the various types of aggregations available to use in the **Data** tab of TSVB. Now, let's move on to understand how to enrich this with the help of the **Group by** option on the same page.

Understanding the Group by dropdown in the Data tab

A very common feature, the **Group by** functionality is used by SQL developers and analysts to group the data per any specific field in the queries. We are going to learn how to do a similar thing in TSVB, where we will use this **Group by** feature to create bucket aggregations by grouping by the data per one field.

Figure 5.11 – The Group by dropdown

As seen in the preceding figure, there are multiple ways to group by the data, such as the following:

- **Filters**: This is used to group the data according to a specific use case category filter. We can select different colors to assign to a specific filter.

- **Terms**: This works on the bucket aggregation giving us the top values of the buckets, which will represent the top values of the field we select in the dropdown.

- **Filter**: This merely gives us the option to create a graph based on a KQL query, which can be used to filter out the documents based on a use case requirement.

We have now come to the point where we can successfully connect our data in the Elasticsearch cluster and create a TSVB visualization by adding values for **Aggregation** and **Group by** in TSVB.

Next, we will dive into the different representations of visualizations such as **Metric**, **Top N**, **Gauge**, **Markdown**, and **Table**, which are still governed by the same **Data** tab aggregations.

Exploring the Metric, Top N, Gauge, Markdown, and Table types of TSVB

With TSVB's intuitive interface and powerful features, analyzing time series data has never been easier. Whether you're tracking performance metrics, monitoring sensor readings, or studying financial trends, TSVB provides a flexible and efficient solution for visualizing and exploring your data.

By default, TSVB displays the full range of data on the y axis, including zero. However, if you want to focus on specific ranges of values, you can easily modify the y axis scale. To do this, simply navigate to **Data** | **Options** | **Fill** and enter 0 in the **Fill** field. This will automatically scale the y axis from the minimum to the maximum values of your data.

The **Metric** type of TSVB offers a feature to create metric visualizations that can be dynamic, as per the recent change in the value of the calculated metrics in the data at any particular moment.

For example, we can calculate two different metrics, as shown in the following screenshot, for the `Kibana_sample_data_ecommerce` sample dataset:

Total Count
1,948
Avg of products price $34.28

Figure 5.12 – The Metric type

In order to get to this output, we would need to fill in the **Data** tab with the values shown as follows:

Figure 5.13 – The Data tab values

One of the key features of TSVB is the ability to apply conditional coloring based on the values of the metrics. This allows users to easily identify anomalies or trends in their data by assigning specific colors to various categories of value in the dataset.

When we navigate to **Panel options** beside the **Data** tab, we can select the color conditional rules.

For example, for any value above 1,900, we can set the background to go black and the text to turn red, as shown in the following figure:

Figure 5.14 – Color conditional rules

This would output something like in the following figure:

Figure 5.15 – The TSVB with color rules applied

This color formatting can be done in the respective **Panel options** tab for all the other types of TSVB as well.

Top N and Gauge

Top N and **Gauge** work in a very similar way as both of them are based on the bucket aggregation output, which will create buckets (horizontal bars in **Top N**, and gauge shapes in **Gauge**). It is an interesting way to visualize how bucketing can help you view the data in the form of different colors, and categories in the form of bars/gauges. The color conditional rule works in the exact same way as we have seen in the **Metric** type of visualization except, this time, your horizontal bars will be colored, as shown in the following figure:

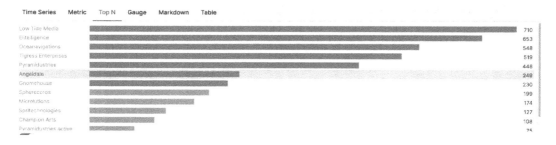

Figure 5.16 – The output of the color conditional rule: Set bar color to red if metric is greater than 200

Similarly for the **Gauge** type in TSVB, for buckets of product manufacturers where the rule is set to turn the gauge blue if the metric is less than 300, the output will be as shown in the following figure:

Figure 5.17 – The buckets of product manufacturers

Markdown and Table

Another useful feature of TSVB is the **Markdown** visualization. This allows users to insert dynamic data using Markdown with the Handlebars syntax, whose documentation is easily accessible from the **Markdown** TSVB page. It also supports custom CSS, which helps users create a custom appearance of the visualizations according to their use case-specific requirements.

For example, if we want to simply write down some text explaining something about a dashboard, then **Markdown** is a great way to do it. In the example shown in the following screenshot, we are introducing the data analytics dashboard with a welcome statement:

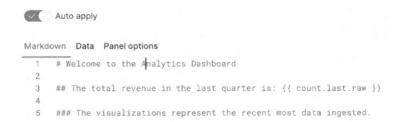

Figure 5.18 – The Markdown type

The very interesting dynamic feature of this TSVB Markdown is that the numeric calculations are represented by an arbitrary expression using the Mustache language, which picks up the most current calculation according to the recent aggregation calculation, meaning that if the data changes, the revenue value in the example would change as well. This is a useful way to display information about the dashboard, which can help build a perspective for users who are not acquainted with the data.

The **Table** type in TSVB is very similar to the data table visualization plus the dynamic features of the color conditionals. Whenever users need to represent the aggregation results against the individual field values, a table visualization is the perfect fit for such use cases.

For example, if we have to build a table on the basis of certain metric calculations and field values, it can be drawn as shown in the following screenshot:

Time Series	Metric	Top N	Gauge	Markdown	Table

order_date ↑	Average of products.base_unit_price	Cardinality of products.price
Jan 11, 2024 @ 17:21:36.000	$26.49	$8.00
Jan 11, 2024 @ 20:38:53.000	$29.49	$6.00
Jan 15, 2024 @ 22:38:24.000	$42.99	$7.00
Jan 16, 2024 @ 06:46:34.000	$36.83	$4.00
Jan 11, 2024 @ 01:34:05.000	$35.24	$4.00
Jan 11, 2024 @ 03:43:41.000	$28.82	$5.00
Jan 11, 2024 @ 04:29:46.000	$38.24	$4.00

Auto apply   The changes will be automatically applie

Figure 5.19 – The Table type

The color conditional rule here is set per column. Hence, the preceding screenshot shows the output for the rule set for the **Cardinality** column where the text will turn to red if the metric number goes above 5. This color change can be dynamic and will change as per the current data in the cluster.

Overall, we have seen that TSVB is a versatile tool that empowers users to analyze time series data in a meaningful way by using different kinds of representations, such as Time Series, Metric, Top N, Gauge, Markdown, and Table. With its rich set of features, easy-to-use functionalities, and intuitive interface, it simplifies the process of exploring and understanding complex temporal datasets. Whether you're tracking business KPIs or observing your business trends, TSVB provides the tools necessary for informed decision-making.

Putting TSVB to use

If we implement TSVB, it is important to note that it has practical applications in various areas, such as the following:

- Trend analysis of multiple index patterns within a single visualization. It allows for complete customization of visualizations, giving users the ability to adjust everything from date formats to color features. This level of customization enables the creation of unique representations.

- TSVB also supports the implementation of color conditional rules, which can be used to represent specific thresholds based on user requirements.

- Additionally, TSVB facilitates the effortless creation of complex calculations by combining basic metric aggregations with pipeline aggregations.

- The tool also offers the use of annotations to highlight significant events in the data's behavior.

- Furthermore, TSVB allows for the comparison of current data with earlier time series data by defining an offset for a second metric.

- Finally, TSVB provides easy visualization options, allowing users to switch between Time Series, Metric, Top N, Gauge, Markdown, and Table views to effectively analyze their data.

A very good example of implementing TSVB is a use case where you have a project threshold/target for a field's value to reach and you wish to represent that with a graph. We can leverage the **Static Value** aggregation for this and create a new time series by clicking the + icon at the extreme right-hand side of the **Data** tab of TSVB, as shown in the following figure:

Figure 5.20 – Navigating to Add Series

Once we add a series, we can select the **Static Value** aggregation from the **Aggregation** dropdown (as explained earlier in this chapter), thereby changing the color and the name of the series. This will create a visualization similar to the following screenshot:

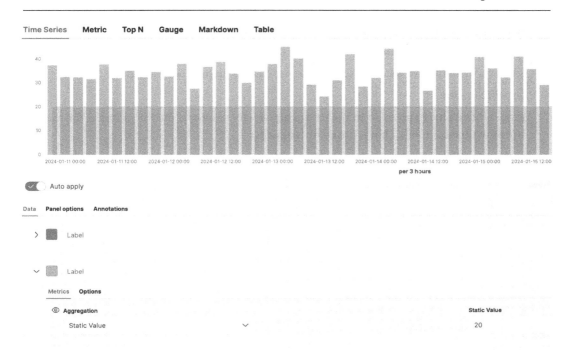

Figure 5.21 – The navigation and the graph created in TSVB, Kibana

As shown in the preceding screenshot, for the visualization created, it is important to notice how the **Static Value** aggregation creates a straight line to represent a target/threshold and the **Total count** series creates another graph in the form of bars for us to gain clarity on whether the data points are able to reach the target or not.

Using Annotations

Have you ever needed a very simple yet easy-to-understand feature to denote a very important event in your dataset on the graph? Guess what? **Annotations** does the trick for you.

For example, if we want to mark an event where the product base price goes above 50, then we can do this by following these very simple steps:

1. Navigate to **TSVB**, and switch to the **Annotations** tab.

2. Go to **Annotations** and add data source as **Data** view. For example, Kibana_sample_data_ecommerce.

3. Select the **Time** field (this can be a timestamp or a data field in your dataset): **order_date**.

4. Enter **Query String**, where we define the rule/condition to be satisfied for the annotation to appear on the graph: **products.base_price > 150**.

5. Select the field that we want to use to create annotations in **product.base_price**.

6. Select **Icon**: bell.

7. Enter a Mustache expression in the Row template, for example, the following in this case: **{{product.base_price}}. (Uses Mustache language)**

The output of these implementation steps should be as follows:

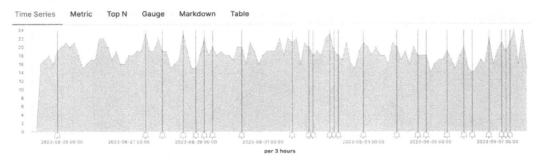

Figure 5.22 – The example of Annotations

As we can see in the preceding screenshot, wherever the graph has an event that results in `true` for the query string statement, we can see the annotations being created at those exact events in the graph. This graph can be then saved and used in any dashboard, which will effectively represent the events being highlighted in near-real time as the data gets ingested in the cluster.

Summary

In this chapter, we understood how TSVB is a very powerful and useful tool that lets us create dynamic and versatile visualizations based on near-real-time data. We studied the **Metric** visualization, which helps us plot metric aggregations in the form of a metric on the visualization and has the dynamic effect of updating color conditionals automatically.

Top N and **Gauge**, on the other hand, focus on the implementation of the bucket aggregation. **Markdown** is a very unique type of visualization that helps us add text or information on any particular use case-specific dashboard. Lastly, the **Table** visualization helps us to visualize the data in tabular format along with the aggregation implementation against individual fields.

In the next chapter, we shall open up new doors to learn how machine learning helps us take this data analysis to an advanced level.

Part 3:
Analytics on a Dashboard

In this part, we will come to understand that the journey through data doesn't end with numbers on a screen. This part is your launchpad to elevate your analysis, where raw information transforms into revelations. With the help of machine learning in Kibana, we will create anomaly detection jobs to bring out the narratives from intricate patterns and hidden connections. We'll equip you with the tools to craft dashboards that dance with data, telling compelling stories and empowering informed decisions. Forget static charts – get ready to paint vibrant landscapes of insight, revealing the unseen dimensions within your data's depths.

This part has the following chapters:

- *Chapter 6, Data Analysis with Machine Learning*
- *Chapter 7, Graph Visualization*
- *Chapter 8, Finally, the Dashboard*

6

Data Analysis with Machine Learning

Machine learning has revolutionized the way we analyze and interpret data. With its advanced algorithms, it has become easier to uncover patterns and trends that were once hidden. One such tool that harnesses the power of machine learning is Kibana. Kibana provides a free Data Visualizer feature, enabling users to gain deeper insights into their data. If your data is stored in Elasticsearch and includes a time field, Data Visualizer can help you identify potential fields for anomaly detection. Anomaly detection is crucial in today's rapidly evolving landscape as it allows us to detect unusual or suspicious activities that may indicate cyberattacks, infrastructure problems, or business issues.

By leveraging machine learning algorithms, Kibana's anomaly detection feature can automatically spot anomalies in your data without the need for extensive human effort. This saves valuable time and resources while ensuring that critical events are promptly identified and addressed. With Kibana's Data Visualizer and machine learning capabilities, businesses can gain a comprehensive understanding of their data, even in large and complex datasets. By detecting anomalies, organizations can proactively respond to potential threats or problems before they escalate. By reducing the burden of manual inspection and rule maintenance, organizations can focus on strategic decision-making and problem-solving.

In this chapter, we shall study three very important aspects of machine learning that are available in the machine learning interface of Kibana:

- Understanding anomaly detection in time series data
- Analyzing data with entity-centric analysis
- Setting up alerts

Technical requirements

As per the basic requirements, we assume that you have data ingested in the cluster and that Elasticsearch and Kibana are set up on the nodes of (any) environment (cloud or local).

Once Kibana is up and running, we can navigate to the **Kibana** home page and choose **Try sample data | Other sample data sets** and click on **Add data for Kibana_sample_data_ecommerce dataset**. We'll be using this dataset to create the visualization on Lens in this chapter.

Understanding anomaly detection in time series data

Anomaly detection is the process of identifying the points in data that don't fit the normal data behavioral patterns. To make this effective, we can automate the whole process. The important point to note here is that this process will be more efficient when the size of the data has increased. The Elastic Stack supports several data analysis use cases that use supervised and unsupervised machine learning, as follows:

- Anomaly detection
- Outlier detection
- Fraud detection
- Forecasting
- Language detection

Our main intention behind putting various techniques to use is to bring out the insights from the most normal-looking data. When we look into anomaly detection, we identify patterns and unusual behavior in the near real-time current and historical data. An unusual data point can be seen in the form of a high spike or very low data behavior, as shown here:

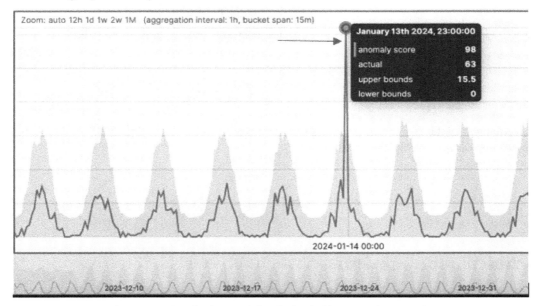

Figure 6.1 – A spike (unusual data behavior) in a sample anomaly detection job in the machine learning app, Kibana

The key terminological terms to keep in mind are as follows:

- **Detector**: This is the combination of an analytical function and the field we are targeting to create a machine learning job

- **Model**: The graph created by an anomaly detection job to depict the usual behavior of the data

- **Influencer field**: The field that we wish to use and that influences (contributes to) the creation of anomalies

Next, we will understand the step-by-step workflow for performing the detection job:

1. The first step is to plan what the workflow of the analysis is going to look like. As per the proprietary machine learning algorithm, the anomalies can be related to time-related deviations in counts and frequencies, statistical rarity, or unusual behavior in geographic data or from a member of a population in the analysis job. According to the dataset that you have, and the type of behavior you wish to detect, you can determine the type of anomaly detection job and begin analysis.

2. The second step is to run the detection job in the machine learning app by selecting the appropriate type of wizard. The following screenshot shows the screen where you can select this:

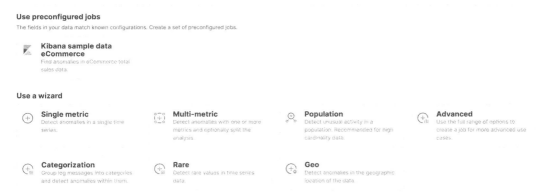

Figure 6.2 – The landing page of the machine learning app, Kibana

Single metric jobs will use a single detector to create a detection job on the dataset we select, whereas **Multi-metric** jobs will have multiple detectors to complete the same process, except the latter is much more efficient in running multiple analyses at the same time.

Population, as we understood earlier, helps you create a job that detects anomalies that are unusual compared to the behavior of the rest of the population. The other wizards can be used to create jobs that log events into categories and use count or rate analytical functions to find anomalies.

When we click on one of the wizards (for example, **Single metric**) and go to the last page to **Create Job**, there are two main result views that you should consider looking into:

- **Single Metric Viewer**: The view of the created anomaly detection job will look something similar to the following:

Single time series analysis of avg transaction_latency (service.name: frontend-node

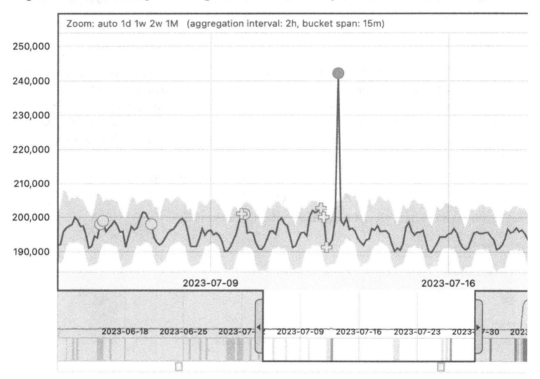

Figure 6.3 – The view of Single Metric Viewer in Kibana

The slider at the bottom of the figure serves as a magnifying glass that will highlight the part of the graph that's been selected by the slider. The red dot on the graph indicates an anomaly; its severity is based on the anomaly score, which is calculated from 0 to 100. If we click on the red dot, it will provide details about the score, as shown in the following screenshot:

Figure 6.4 – The dialog box that appears after clicking the anomaly in Kibana

As we can see, the score is **98**, which is considered a pretty high score. The higher the value, the more severe the anomaly is. If we scroll down on the viewer, we'll see details about the exact events due to which these anomalies are happening in the data. This is great to have when you plan to do a deep root analysis on the data events causing the concerning spikes or lows.

- **Anomaly Explorer**: This view will consolidate all the anomalies that have been found in the whole job and summarize them in this window. On the left-hand side of the view is a list of all the top influencer field values regarding the detected anomalies. This contains the anomalies with maximum scores, where the swim lanes depict the respective values of the influencer field. To see this in action, check out the view of Anomaly Explorer shown in the following screenshot:

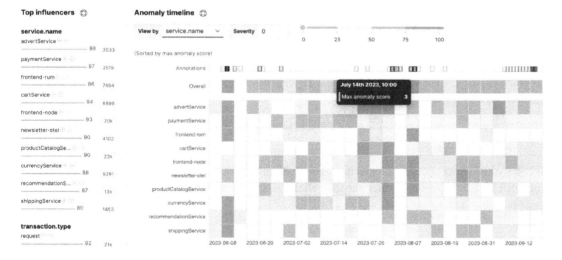

Figure 6.5 – Anomaly Explorer in Kibana

In this section, we learned how anomaly detection helps us detect unusual behaviors and how we can create a job that shows all the meaningful insights in the form of Single Metric Viewer and a consolidated view of the same in the form of Anomaly Explorer.

Now, let's learn how entity-centric analysis helps us modify the analysis process in a specific direction of a use case.

However, there are ample use cases out there that have some *anticipated* traffic coming in in the near future. For example, an e-commerce website that has Elasticsearch and Kibana behind it might have a huge influx of documents at the time of festivities toward the end of the year since people would like to shop a bit more at that time. For example, we could go ahead and add events such as Black Friday or Cyber Monday as events that occur every year. These would normally be reflected as "abnormal" behavior in the data unless we add them to the calendar and let Kibana know that something like this is set to happen. This is where we can use the calendar API. We can create this API as follows:

```
PUT _ml/calendars/<calendar_id>/jobs/<job_id>
```

Upon implementing this in the dev console, we'll receive a response similar to the following:

```
{
    "calendar_id": "Festival-season-influx",
    "job_ids": [
        machine-learning-task"
    ]
}
```

Here, the calendar ID can be any string that represents a unique name for the calendar event and the job ID can be the name of the anomaly detection job that has been predicted to have unusual behavior and needs to be added to the calendar.

Retaining too many of these can also be an overhead for the cluster, which makes it increasingly important to discard these as needed. The DELETE calendar API can help you do this. It can be implemented as follows:

```
DELETE _ml/calendars/<calendar_id>/events/<event_id>
```

This helps you discard or delete the specific calendar event with that event ID and calendar ID. However, if you wish to delete the whole calendar with all the IDs, the following API will come to the rescue:

```
DELETE _ml/calendars/<calendar_id>
```

Once we receive a response similar to the following, we know that the task has been completed successfully:

```
{
    "acknowledged": true

}
```

Moreover, when we talk about future events, it is always a good idea to know a little bit about what's coming. For example, if there is an underlying pattern of the log rate dropping every last Friday of the month, once forecasted, a user can rectify that event since it is going to happen soon. This is where the forecast feature of machine learning steps in. It can be done through a DSL query, like so:

```
POST _ml/anomaly_detectors/<job_id>/_forecast
```

It can also be done by clicking the Forecast button in Single Metric Viewer, as shown in the following screenshot:

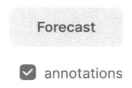

Figure 6.6 – The Forecast feature in Kibana

This requires the `manage_ml` privilege; if a cluster does not have that, a user might not be able to run the forecast as it would return the following error:

Figure 6.7 – Error message when using the Forecast feature in Kibana

The **Forecast** feature leverages your historical data to predict trends and potential anomalies. Think of it as a crystal ball powered by algorithms, giving you a glimpse into what might lie ahead.

Imagine forecasting website traffic to optimize server resources, predicting equipment failures to schedule proactive maintenance, or even anticipating spikes in customer demand to adjust marketing campaigns. Forecast empowers you to make proactive decisions, not just react to what's happened. As an example, if you want to forecast a week in advance, you would need to have a week of historical data, and so on. It's like an automated analyst, tirelessly chewing through data, identifying patterns, and spitting out probability curves.

Let's understand this by considering a real-time market use case.

Imagine a bustling e-commerce platform during a massive holiday sale. Orders are pouring in, and excitement is palpable. But amid the chaos, the team knows that even a momentary downtime could spell disaster. This is where Kibana machine learning steps in as a vigilant guardian:

- **Real-time anomaly detection**: Kibana continuously analyzes server metrics such as response times, database query rates, and error logs. The moment a metric spikes or deviates from normal patterns, it triggers an alert. Engineers are instantly notified, allowing them to quickly investigate and address potential issues before customers experience any glitches.

- **Predictive forecasting**: Machine learning models analyze historical sales patterns and anticipate future trends. This enables the team to proactively scale server resources, optimize inventory levels, and adjust marketing campaigns to match anticipated demand in real time.

- **Personalized customer experiences**: Kibana's machine learning capabilities can even power product recommendations and tailored content based on shoppers' real-time behavior. This creates a more engaging and relevant experience for each customer, boosting sales and satisfaction.

As the sale progresses, Kibana machine learning proves its worth:

- It catches a sudden spike in database query times, prompting the team to quickly optimize queries and prevent slowdowns

- It flags a potential fraud attempt based on unusual purchase patterns, allowing the security team to intervene and protect customer data

- It predicts a surge in traffic for a specific product category, enabling the marketing team to launch targeted ads and drive additional sales

Thanks to Kibana machine learning, the sale concludes as a resounding success. Customers can now enjoy a seamless shopping experience, the team can celebrate averted crises, and the platform can reap the rewards of proactive, data-driven decision-making in real time.

In this section, we learned how we can create an anomaly detection job and inculcate the use of various APIs to serve very specific use cases. Now, let's understand how things work under the hood by learning how the algorithm works.

How does the machine learning algorithm work?

Elastic's machine learning operates by utilizing advanced algorithms to analyze and interpret patterns within large datasets, enabling users to uncover meaningful insights and anomalies in their data. It employs various machine learning techniques, including anomaly detection, regression analysis, and clustering, to discern trends and relationships that may not be immediately apparent.

Moreover, the machine learning model simplifies this process by automating the detection of anomalies or deviations from expected behavior, thereby aiding users in identifying critical issues or opportunities. This powerful tool within the Elastic Stack also provides visualization features to represent the detected patterns, making it user-friendly and accessible. Additionally, Kibana machine learning is designed to adapt and learn from data patterns over time, ensuring continuous improvement and accurate analysis in dynamic environments.

Analyzing data with entity-centric analysis

The feature of Elastic's machine learning entity-centric analytics allows you to analyze your data by utilizing algorithms for classification, outlier detection, and regression. It also enables you to generate new indices that include the results alongside your original data.

If you possess a license that includes machine learning features, you can create jobs for entity-centric analytics and view the outcomes on the **Data Frame Analytics** page in Kibana. The key features that help with this type of analysis are transforms and DataFrame analytics.

Let's understand both.

Transforms

Transforms are specific implementations that are used to convert typical time series data into entity-centric data so that we can categorize the data into specific entities. We can do this by creating new indices with summarized data in them. Transforms work by helping us leverage their continuous mode functionality, where we can not only work with time series data that is coming in batches but also continuous real-time data.

Transforms can be of two types: pivot and latest.

Let's say we have an index where the following type of sample data is coming in:

Date	Name	Customer Id
02-2-2023	Owen Mills	5
23-5-2023	Micheal James	4
4-5-6-2022	Owen Mills	1
3-8-2022	Micheal James	9

Figure 6.8 – A sample of the time series dataset

The preceding table can be converted into entity-centric data, as follows:

Name	Customer id
Owen Mills	6
Micheal James	13

Figure 6.9 – The table after being converted into entity-centric data

When using transforms in Elasticsearch, you can define a pivot. A pivot is essentially a set of features that will transform your index into a new format that is easier to understand and analyze.

To define a pivot, the first step is to select the fields that you want to use to group your data. These fields can be categorical (terms) or numerical. If you choose to use numerical fields, the values will be bucketed based on an interval that you specify. The process of defining a pivot allows you to organize and structure your data in a way that makes it more meaningful, thereby providing insights into the relationships between different variables and helping identify patterns or trends within your dataset. This can be particularly useful when you're working with large datasets or when you're trying to analyze complex information. Observability data, once a tangled web of metrics and logs, has a new ally: pivot transforms. As we have seen, these clever tools unlock hidden insights by reshaping data, giving you a bird's-eye view of your system's health.

Think of it like taking a kaleidoscope to a jumble of colored beads. Pivots rearrange those beads, revealing patterns you wouldn't see otherwise. Aggregate across timestamps, group by service names, or slice data by custom fields – the possibilities are endless. Suddenly, you can spot trends such as rising error rates in specific regions, identify resource bottlenecks affecting service performance, or even trace back anomalies to their root causes. Pivot transforms turn raw data into actionable intelligence, empowering you to optimize performance, troubleshoot issues faster, and ultimately ensure a smooth-running system.

In summary, pivoting with transforms in Elasticsearch enables you to reformat your index and obtain a summarized view of your data. It allows for better organization, analysis, and interpretation of your data, leading to more informed decision-making and improved outcomes.

DataFrame analytics

DataFrame analytics is a powerful feature in Kibana machine learning that allows you to analyze complex datasets and gain valuable insights. With the help of Kibana, you can easily visualize and explore your data in a user-friendly manner.

This concept can be subdivided into implementing three things:

- **Outlier detection**: One important aspect of data analysis is outlier detection, which helps identify data points that deviate from the norm. By pinpointing these anomalies, you can investigate the reasons behind their abnormal behavior and take appropriate actions.

- **Regression**: Regression analysis enables you to estimate relationships between different fields in your dataset. This allows you to make predictions based on these relationships, helping you uncover patterns and trends in your data.

- **Classification**: Classification algorithms play a crucial role in predicting the class or category of a given data point. By training these algorithms on existing labeled data, you can accurately classify new instances based on their features. All these techniques, when combined, provide a comprehensive approach to analyzing and interpreting data effectively.

Hence, we can discover hidden insights, uncover patterns, and reveal meaningful stories through flexible calculations and aggregations to derive impactful decision making.

The DataFrame Analytics API

The DataFrame Analytics API can be leveraged to enhance your data by incorporating additional insights through the application of machine learning algorithms. To work in this direction, it is essential to understand how the API designed for it works.

The DataFrame Analytics API generates a job that conducts an analysis on source indices and stores the outcome in a specified destination index.

In cases where the destination index is not present, it is automatically generated upon initiation of the job. The DataFrame Analytics API has the flexibility to be initiated and halted multiple times during its life cycle. In instances where the destination index is already in existence, it is utilized as-is. Consequently, there is the option to preconfigure the destination index with customized settings and mappings. Upon the initial execution of the DataFrame Analytics API, if the destination index does not already exist, it is automatically created. The settings for the destination index, such as **number_of_shards** and **number_of_replicas**, are replicated from the source. In the scenario of multiple source indices, the destination index adopts the highest setting values. Additionally, mappings for the destination index are duplicated from the indices coming from the source. In the presence of mapping conflicts, the jobs won't be able to be initiated.

It is also important to note that when Elasticsearch security features are active/enabled, the DataFrame Analytics API retains information about who initiated the job and ran it with the help of the credentials being used. We have seen that visualizing data through DataFrame Analytics is the most effective method for comprehending its significance. By utilizing dashboards, you can transform your data, whether it be from a single or multiple perspectives, into a compilation of panels that provide a clear understanding of the data. These panels not only convey a narrative about your data but also enable you to take a deep dive into the data that is relevant to you. Furthermore, DataFrame Analytics will help you take this implementation a notch higher, thereby leveraging all the key insights from your data that might have been obscured otherwise. To start the DataFrame Analytics job from scratch, you can create a **domain specific language (DSL)** query on the dev console with the PUT method, as follows:

```
PUT _ml/data_frame/analytics/<data_frame_analytics_id>
```

However, the cluster does require some prerequisites before we implement this DSL query:

- The source indices must be present in the cluster – for example, **read index** and **view_ index_metadata**
- The destination indices must also be present in the cluster – for example, **read, index, manage**, and **create_index**
- The user implementing the query must have admin privileges via **machine_learning_admin role**

APIs to implement to know more about machine learning

For any task that is being implemented, and you need to know more about what is happening under the hood, we have several GET method APIs that work based on a DSL query.

For example, GET _ml/info will return the result of the current machine learning jobs on the cluster.

On the other hand, if you're keen to dig into the statistics of the node information concerning machine learning jobs, then APIs such as the ones listed here can be of tremendous help:

```
GET _ml/memory/<node_id>/_stats
GET _ml/memory/_stats
```

These not only provide information about the JVM heap being used by the machine learning modes but also throw some light on how memory consumption is being done on individual nodes. Don't forget that implementing this DSL query requires the **monitor_ml** cluster privilege in the respective built-in roles in Kibana.

The factors that contribute to the time taken in running a ML job are the volume of data points in the dataset, the number of fields considered in the analysis, the advanced configuration options provided, and the nature of the analytics. Consequently, in most scenarios, there is no universal time in which the jobs finish running. It can be from a few seconds to a few hours, and this can be tackled by starting the large dataset points with a low percentage of training. Now, let's learn how we can have the implementation communicate through alerts when anything out of the ordinary happens in our dataset.

Setting up alerts

Kibana's alerting capabilities go beyond the basics, incorporating support for machine learning rules. These rules allow you to schedule checks that can detect anomalies in one or more anomaly detection jobs.

Additionally, they can assess the health of a job based on specific conditions. When the conditions of a rule are met, Kibana creates an alert and triggers the associated action. This integration of machine learning with alerting in Kibana enhances the platform's ability to proactively identify and respond to potential issues or abnormal patterns in data. By leveraging machine learning algorithms, Kibana empowers users to automate the monitoring process and improve overall operational efficiency.

With its advanced alerting features, Kibana provides organizations with a powerful tool for staying ahead of potential problems and optimizing their data analysis workflows.

The Kibana platform offers a range of powerful machine learning capabilities to enhance your data analysis and monitoring processes. One such capability is the anomaly detection alert, which allows you to identify anomalies in your data based on specified rule conditions. By leveraging the advanced algorithms and models within Kibana, you can effectively pinpoint any unexpected patterns or outliers that may require further investigation.

Additionally, Kibana allows you to monitor the health of your anomaly detection jobs. This feature ensures that any operational issues that could potentially hinder the job's performance in detecting anomalies are promptly flagged to you by an action that you can set up. For example, you can create a rule to check an anomaly job every 20 minutes for use case-specific critical anomalies and have it notify you through an email or Slack message.

Let's look at an example so that we know how to create a rule for an anomaly detection job:

1. Navigate to the Kibana home page and choose **Stack Management | Alerts and Insights | Rules**.

2. Click on the **Create rule** option, as shown here:

Create your first rule

Receive an alert through email, Slack, or another connector
when a condition is met.

Figure 6.10 – The first step in creating rules

3. Enter the details about the rule, including its name, the time interval in which you need to run the rule, and the rest as per the specifics of the use case. The following screenshot shows the details you will need to fill in:

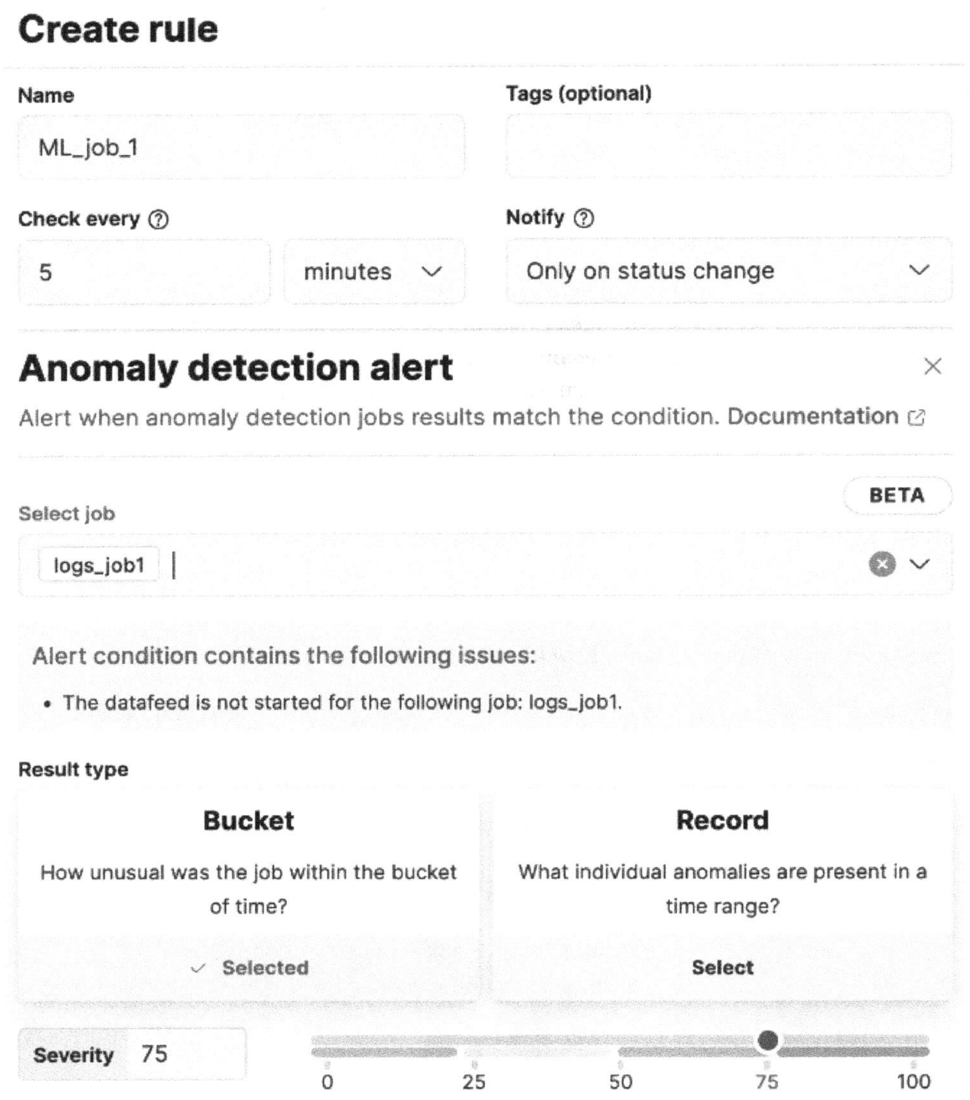

Create rule

Name

ML_job_1

Tags (optional)

Check every ⑦

5   minutes ⌄

Notify ⑦

Only on status change   ⌄

Anomaly detection alert   ✕

Alert when anomaly detection jobs results match the condition. **Documentation** ⌕

Select job   BETA

logs_job1 | ⊗ ⌄

Alert condition contains the following issues:

- The datafeed is not started for the following job: logs_job1.

Result type

Bucket	**Record**
How unusual was the job within the bucket of time?	What individual anomalies are present in a time range?
✓ Selected	Select

Severity 75   ●

0   25   50   75   100

Figure 6.11 – The second step in creating rules and connectors

Finally, we can set up an action that tells us when the rule is satisfied. For this, we must navigate to the Kibana home page and choose **Stack Management | Alerts and Insights | Connectors**.

The **Connectors** page is shown in the following screenshot:

Connectors

Connectors

Connect third-party software with your alerting data.

Connectors   **Logs**

Create connector   Q Search...   Type ∨

Name	Type	Compatibility	
Demo emails	Email	Alerting Rules	PRECONFIGURED ▷

Rows per page: 10 ∨   ‹ 1 ›

Figure 6.12 – The Connectors page in Kibana

Upon clicking the **Create connector** button, we can view the list of different connectors that can be selected as a part of the action that gets triggered once the rule is satisfied:

Select a connector

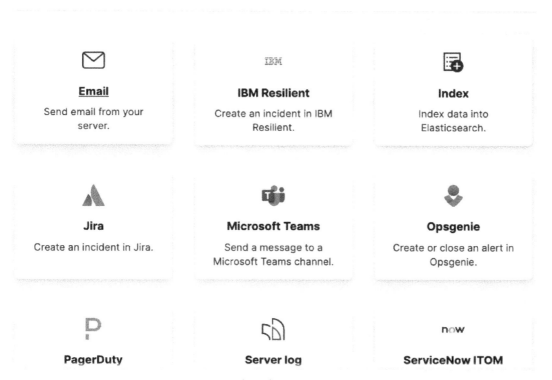

Figure 6.13 – The Select a connector page

Now, we can follow the steps provided and create a connector that will be visible in the table on the **Connectors** page (as depicted in *Figure 6.12*).

In this section, we understood the process of setting up alerts for an anomaly detection job concerning machine learning in Kibana. The same alerting can not only be used for the machine learning app but also for the overall Elasticsearch resource alerting process and many other performance-tuning use cases.

Summary

In this chapter, we understood the extensive features and capabilities that Kibana's machine learning provides, thereby leveraging the big data in your systems to find some meaningful business insights to help the use case.

Then, we saw how anomalies can be deemed unusual behavior, even in the most normal-looking data. This helps us be aware of and predict potentially alarming events in the future. Moreover, we saw how the alerting mechanism in Kibana helps provide some great findings for the data analysis process.

With Kibana's comprehensive suite of machine learning functionalities, you can streamline your data analysis workflow and stay proactive in identifying potential issues or anomalies in your datasets. Whether it's identifying anomalies, monitoring job health, or leveraging other advanced analytics capabilities, Kibana enables users to unlock valuable insights from their data and drive meaningful business outcomes. In the next chapter, we will take a look at a very interesting type of visualization called Graph that can help us build a view for establishing relationships between two or more fields in a dataset.

7

Graph Visualization

The capabilities of graph analytics allow you to uncover the relationships between items within an Elasticsearch index. By examining the connections between indexed terms, you can identify the most significant associations. This functionality has a wide range of applications, including fraud detection and recommendation engines.

For instance, through graph exploration, you can reveal the specific website vulnerabilities that hackers are targeting, empowering you to strengthen your website's security. Additionally, you can leverage graph-based personalized recommendations to enhance the shopping experience for your e-commerce customers. It relies solely on shared values between documents to establish connections, enabling the creation of an interconnected network of related terms within the index.

We are going to look into the following key concepts relating to how graphs are created, configured, and troubleshooted when necessary:

- Creating a graph
- Customizing a graph
- Troubleshooting a graph

Technical requirements

As far as basic requirements go, we assume that you have data ingested in the cluster and Elasticsearch and Kibana are set up on the nodes in the environment (cloud or local).

Once Kibana is up and running, we can navigate to the Kibana home page and then to **Try sample data**. Then, select **Other sample data sets** and click on the **Add data for Kibana_sample_data_ ecommerce** dataset and **Kibana_sample_data_logs**. We will be using these datasets to create the graph visualization in this chapter.

Creating a graph

The Graph API offers an alternative method for retrieving and summarizing data about the documents and keywords in your Elasticsearch index. Essentially, a graph represents a network of interconnected elements. In our context, this refers to a network of related keywords within the index.

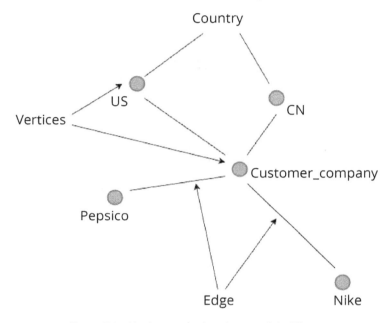

Figure 7.1 – Vertices and edges in a graph in Kibana

The keywords that you wish to include in the graph are referred to as **vertices**. Each connection between two vertices represents a relationship. This relationship summarizes the documents that contain both of the terms associated with the vertices. The terms that have been indexed serve as the graph vertices. By utilizing Elasticsearch aggregations, the connections are generated dynamically. The API utilizes **Elasticsearch relevance scoring** to identify the most significant connections. This means that the same data structures and relevance-ranking tools used for text searches in Elasticsearch are employed by the Graph API to distinguish valuable signals from the usual noise found in connected data.

To uncover the connections within your data, let's see how to create a graph step by step, as follows:

1.   Access the primary menu and navigate to the **Graph** option, as shown:

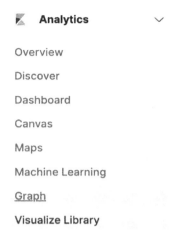

Figure 7.2 – The primary menu in Kibana

2. If you are unfamiliar with Kibana and lack any existing data, click on the link shown in the following screenshot to incorporate sample data. This example utilizes the Kibana sample web logs dataset:

Figure 7.3 – Sample data logs graph in Kibana

Choose the specific data source you wish to investigate.

Kibana will then generate graphs that illustrate the relationships among the most prominent fields in your selected data source.

The following screenshot shows the final representation view of a graph visualization after it is created using the **agent.keyword**, **extension.keyword**, **geo.src**, and **response.keyword** fields on the sample dataset, **Kibana Sample Data - Data Logs**:

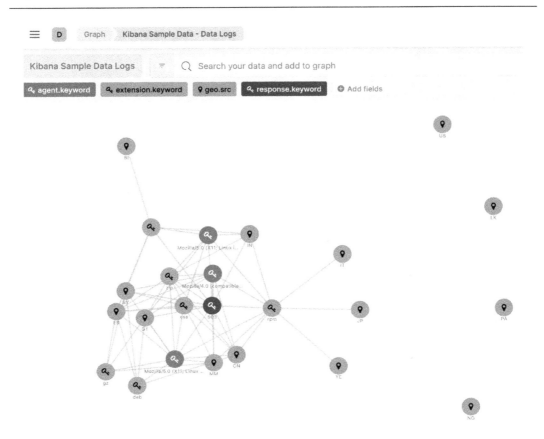

Figure 7.4 – Sample graph created for logs data in Kibana

A key thing to note here is the points where we click any edge connecting the two vertices will tell us what the common documents between the two vertices are. In the following figure, we are clicking on the edge between the **Men's Clothing** and **Asia** vertices:

Figure 7.5 – Graph for e-commerce data focused on the edge of the vertices

A Venn diagram will display, showing us the common points, as in the following screenshot:

Figure 7.6 – Venn diagram for common documents shared between the two vertices

Graphs are crucial in many use cases to depict the relationships between entities.

It is easy to become overwhelmed by the vast amounts of data we have and get lost in the intricate details hidden within terabytes of logs. However, analysts must have the ability to navigate through this sea of information and uncover insights that offer fresh warnings, understanding, or perspectives. Kibana graphs offer a means of communication that effectively presents the interconnected nodes and links within our data, making them easily understandable. Let's now look at tweaking features to customize graphs.

Customizing a graph

We can customize the appearance of vertices in our graphs by applying personalized colors and icons. Additionally, we have the ability to configure the number of vertices that are added to the graph during a search operation. We can also block certain terms and do many more things.

Each vertex in the graph is associated with a color, icon, and label. If you wish to modify the color or icon for all vertices within a specific category, locate the style icon in the control bar and click on it, as shown in the following screenshot:

Figure 7.7 – Styling options for vertices in graphs in Kibana

By default, the graph feature is designed to filter out unnecessary noise from your data. However, if this default setting does not align with your specific dataset, you have the option to make adjustments. Simply navigate to the **Settings** menu and select **Advanced settings**. From there, you can fine-tune how the graph queries your data, ensuring that it presents only the most relevant results, which also improves the overall performance. For more detailed instructions, refer to the *Troubleshooting a graph* section. Upon navigating to **Advanced settings**, as mentioned previously, you will see the following:

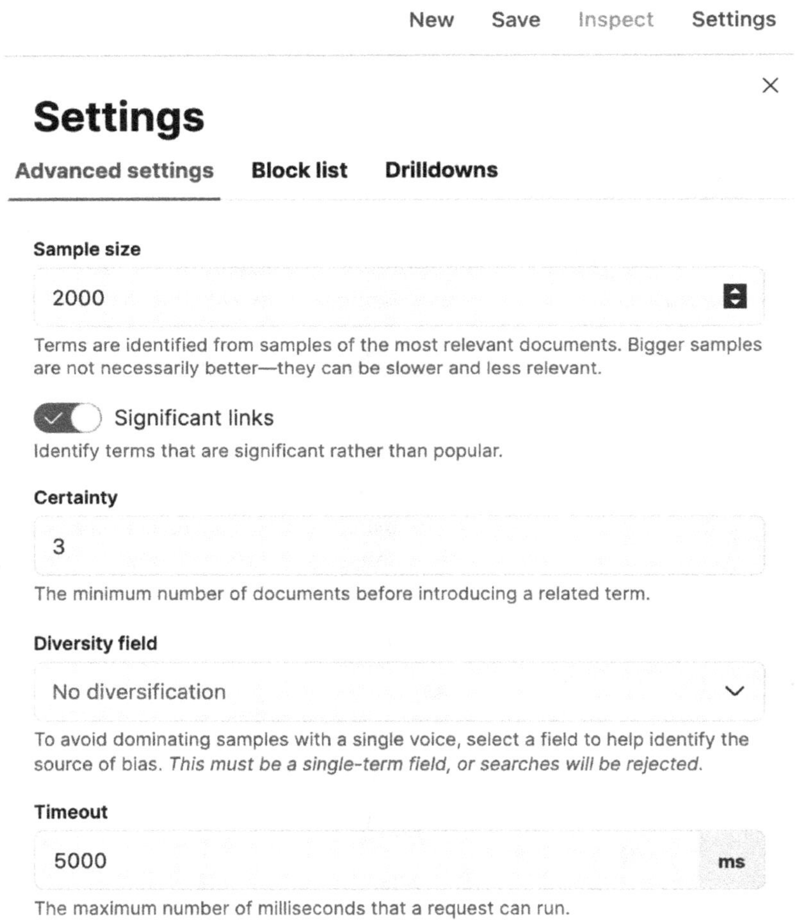

New   Save   Inspect   Settings

×

Settings

Advanced settings   **Block list**   **Drilldowns**

Sample size

2000

Terms are identified from samples of the most relevant documents. Bigger samples are not necessarily better—they can be slower and less relevant.

Significant links
Identify terms that are significant rather than popular.

Certainty

3

The minimum number of documents before introducing a related term.

Diversity field

No diversification

To avoid dominating samples with a single voice, select a field to help identify the source of bias. *This must be a single-term field, or searches will be rejected.*

Timeout

5000   ms

The maximum number of milliseconds that a request can run.

Figure 7.8 – Advanced settings tab for a graph in Kibana

Furthermore, you can customize the number of vertices that are added to the graph during a search or expand operation. By default, only the top five most relevant terms for each field are included at a time to prevent overcrowding. Should you wish to increase this number, click on a specific field, choose **Edit settings**, and modify the value for **Terms per hop**.

Blocked terms are not permitted in the graph. To prevent a term from appearing, choose the corresponding vertex and click on the Block icon in the graph toolbar. If you wish to view a list of blocked terms, navigate to **Settings** and select **Blocked terms**.

The graph utilizes a **force layout** mechanism, where vertices act as magnets and repel each other. By default, when you add a new vertex to the graph, all vertices will start moving. In certain cases, this movement may continue for some time. To lock a vertex in its current position, click on the Pause icon in the graph toolbar.

To access the drilldown buttons for the selected vertices, click on the Drilldown icon in the graph toolbar. For Drilldown configuration, go to **Settings** and select **Drilldowns**. You can also disable the drilldown configuration if desired.

Drilldowns allow you to view additional information about a selected vertex in a new browser window. For instance, you can set up a drill-down URL to perform a web search for the selected vertex term.

We've learned in detail how you can create a graph and configure the ways to manipulate the fields and values in order to get the exact visualization you intend to build. In the next section, we will learn how troubleshooting works for graphs in Kibana.

Troubleshooting a graph

If you face a simple error of the results not appearing, then the first step is to be mindful of how the Graph API requests are designed to filter out irrelevant result documents by implementing various techniques. Let's look into a few common issues and some strategies to tackle them.

Performance-related issues

To enhance the performance of the graph visualization, the Graph API incorporates a background frequency check for the terms it discovers during exploration. By default, each unique term requires a lookup in the index, which incurs a disk seek and can be costly. However, if noise filtering is not necessary, you can disable this check by setting the **Use significance** parameter to **false**. This eliminates the expensive frequency checks but also means that no quality filtering will be performed on the terms.

If your data contains noise and you need to filter based on significance, there are several strategies you can employ to reduce the number of frequency checks, including the following:

- Increase the frequency threshold. Since many terms occur infrequently, even a slight adjustment to the frequency threshold can significantly decrease the number of candidate terms that need to be checked for their background frequencies.

- The quality of documents that match varies significantly, so you can reduce the sample size.

We want to avoid getting noisy JSON documents that contain too many terms, to improve the overall effectiveness. This can be achieved by either prioritizing shorter documents in the top-results sample through ranking or by actively excluding large documents with your seed and guiding queries.

Finding out whether there are any missing results

The default configurations in Graph API requests are designed to filter out irrelevant results by implementing the following strategies:

- Examining only a subset of the most pertinent documents for a given query
- Considering only terms that exhibit a significant statistical correlation with the selected subset
- Establishing connections between terms based on at least three supporting documents

These default settings are effective in obtaining a general overview from noisy data. However, they may overlook specific details contained within individual documents. If you require a thorough forensic analysis, you can adjust the following settings to ensure that a graph exploration yields all relevant data:

- To obtain more extensive data from each shard, you can enhance `sample_size` for analysis of a greater number of documents
- By disabling the `use_significance` setting, you can retrieve terms without depending on their statistical correlation with the sample
- Lastly, when setting `min_doc_count` for vertices to 1, relationships will be established based on a single document rather than taking into account a set of different relevant documents

By customizing these settings, you can enhance the depth and accuracy of your analysis, allowing you to uncover valuable insights from your data.

Key points for supporting data from multiple indices

The Graph API possesses the ability to examine different indices, types, or aliases through a single API request. Nevertheless, it is crucial to acknowledge that this feature operates under the assumption that each hop done by the API is querying an identical set of indices. Regrettably, currently, it is not feasible to extract a term from one field in an index and employ that value to investigate connections in a distinct field located in another type or index.

One scenario where this could be beneficial is when an index named `hostlogs12435` has an IP address found in the `client_host` field. It may be necessary to investigate whether the same address exists in the `host_ip` field of another index called `savedattacks`.

To enable this functionality, additional mappings would be needed to establish a connection between the values in the `client_host` field of the `hostlogs` index and the `host_ip` field of the `threats` index. Although this functionality isn't currently available, promising avenues for future development are on the horizon. ES|QL holds the potential to enable this capability, and data enrichment through ingest pipelines during data entry offers an alternative approach. If this functionality aligns with your use case, exploring these pathways is certainly worthwhile.

It is important to consider that each of these choices narrows down the range of information examined and may enhance the likelihood of overlooking potentially intriguing details. However, the data that is omitted usually pertains to documents of lesser quality and less frequently used terms, which can be deemed an acceptable compromise.

So, we now understand the concept of troubleshooting graphs. We learned how different performance-related issues could hinder the successful operation of graph visualization. The strategies mentioned can help us not only mitigate these issues but also prevent them from happening in the future.

Summary

In this chapter, we explored how the graph analytics features offer a user-friendly yet robust graph exploration API, along with an interactive graph visualization app designed for Kibana. Best of all, these features seamlessly integrate with existing Elasticsearch indices, eliminating the need for any additional data storage. We learned how to create graph visualization from existing data views as well as reviewing key points to note when it comes to performance tuning and troubleshooting graph visualization.

If you're waiting to learn something really new and super interesting, the next chapter will do that. ES|QL is here to help us get the best out of the search functionality of Kibana. We will also learn about some advanced concepts, such as scripted fields, in Kibana.

Finally, the Dashboard

If you're sitting there wondering when we are really going to connect the pieces to finally see everything on one single glass of pane, then now is that time. We have the dashboard – an interface that helps us put all the puzzle pieces together – and we will finally draw out some insights and conclusions from it. As we know, visualizing data is the most effective method to understand its significance. By utilizing dashboards, you can transform your data, whether it is from a single or multiple perspectives, into a compilation of views that provide a clear understanding of the insights from the data. These views not only convey a narrative about the data but also enable you to concentrate solely on the data that holds relevance for you at any particular point in time.

Let's start looking into kickstarting the process of creating a dashboard, where we explore how it allows you to design, edit, and observe personalized dashboards. Dashboards enable you to merge multiple visualizations onto one page and apply filters, by entering search queries or selecting filters through the visualization elements.

By learning how to share dashboards, we can understand how they will prove valuable for gaining insights into your logs and identifying connections between different visualizations and logs.

Let's move on to understanding how we take the first step of creating a dashboard and then take it forward to explore it further:

- Exploring sample dashboards
- Creating a dashboard from scratch
- Sharing the dashboard

Technical requirements

As per the basic requirements, we assume that you have data ingested in the cluster and that Elasticsearch and Kibana are set up on the nodes of (any) environment (the cloud or locally).

Once Kibana is up and running, we can navigate to the Kibana home page, select **Try sample data**, select **Other sample data sets**, click on **Add data for the Kibana_sample_data_ecommerce** dataset, and then select **Kibana_sample_data_logs**.

Exploring sample dashboards

Delving into the world of Kibana dashboards is like embarking on a treasure hunt for insights. Luckily, you don't have to start with an empty map! Check out the **Sample Dashboards** section within Kibana – it's a goldmine of pre-built visualizations waiting to be explored.

Imagine peeking at a dashboard titled **[Logs] Web Traffic**, as shown in *Figure 8.2*. A time series graph might showcase daily visitor trends, while a pie chart paints a picture of the top referring sources. You can click on segments to drill down further, uncovering specific campaigns or landing pages driving traffic. Kibana, as we have seen, is not just a tool for centralizing data and metrics; it also offers very interesting ways to explore and analyze that data. With its intuitive interface and powerful features, Kibana allows technical leads to quickly pinpoint the cause of spike alerts being triggered within their organization. They can easily drill down into data to identify any patterns or anomalies that may contribute to the alerts. Conversely, business intelligence specialists can leverage Kibana to gain insights into product profitability by creating customized dashboards. They can visualize key metrics such as sales revenue, profit margins, and customer satisfaction scores with it. This also enables them to identify which products are performing well and make informed decisions about resource allocation or pricing strategies.

Furthermore, a dashboard can integrate with other data sources, allowing organizations to centralize data from every corner of their operation. This means that users can access a holistic view of their organization's performance and make data-driven decisions based on real-time insights.

Once we ingest the sample data, we can go on to explore the sample dashboards created by Kibana on the following path – **Home | Main Menu | Analytics | Dashboards**.

The following screenshot shows the Kibana view with sample dashboards:

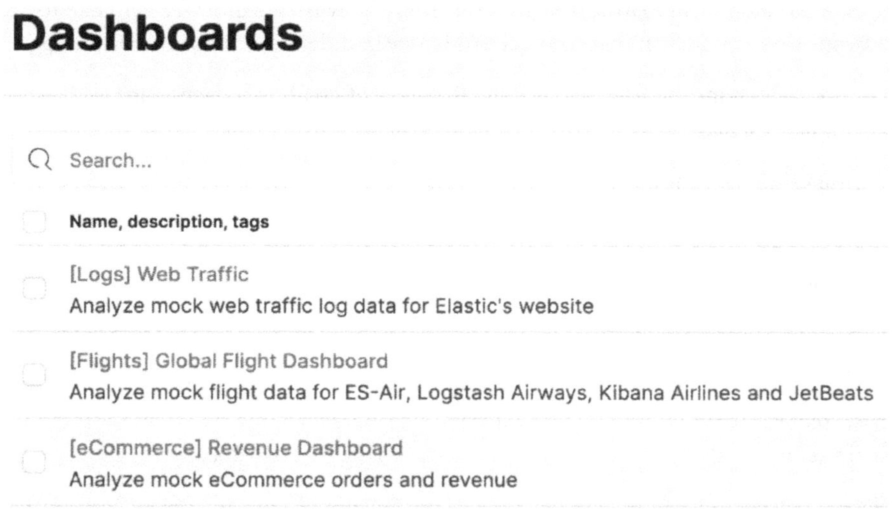

Dashboards

Q Search...

Name, description, tags

[Logs] Web Traffic
Analyze mock web traffic log data for Elastic's website

[Flights] Global Flight Dashboard
Analyze mock flight data for ES-Air, Logstash Airways, Kibana Airlines and JetBeats

[eCommerce] Revenue Dashboard
Analyze mock eCommerce orders and revenue

Figure: 8.1 – An example of the Dashboards main menu in Kibana

When you click on the **[Logs] Web Traffic** dashboard, it shows the various visualizations with diverse representations collected in one view. There are insights from the logs dataset, which include a response code, URL codes, and host IP and client IP information. If we look at the top, we can see that it has a query filter bar, which helps us filter the data on the dashboard using the Kibana Query Language. Furthermore, we also have filters that can be used as an alternative to the query bar.

The following screenshot depicts a view where certain filters are selected, and the **[Logs] Web Traffic** dashboard reflects the updated changes as per the filters:

Figure: 8.2 – The screenshot shows the sample [Logs] Web Traffic dashboard in Kibana

If we click the **Edit** button in the top-right corner, we can edit the dashboard and add/delete visualizations from it.

To add a visualization, we can simply click the **Add from library** button and select one or more saved visualizations from the library to add them to the dashboard. They will be added to the end of the dashboard; hence, you might need to scroll down the page in order to view them. The following screenshots show the step-by-step process to do this.

Figure 8.3 – The first step to edit the dashboard in Kibana

The second step is to add the intended visualization from the library. If you do not have that, you can directly navigate to the **Create visualization** option on the same page (as shown in *Figure 8.8*).

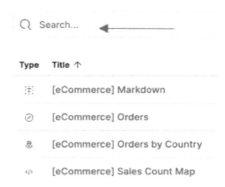

Figure 8.4 – The second step to edit the dashboard in Kibana

The final step is to save the dashboard with the updated changes that you have made so far. Until you save it, the visualization in the Kibana library will not reflect the most recent changes; hence, it is very important to save the dashboard.

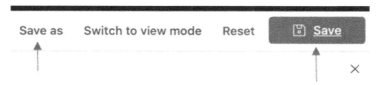

Figure 8.5 – The third and final step to edit the dashboard in Kibana

Once this is done, a popup confirming the dashboard has been saved will appear, as follows:

Figure 8.6 – The fourth step to edit the dashboard in Kibana

In this section, we provided an example of how visualizations of different representations can be brought together on a single page to form a dashboard. Moreover, we also saw the steps to edit this dashboard if required.

Let's now move on to creating our own dashboard from the ground up for any custom requirements, as per the use case.

Creating a dashboard from scratch

With Kibana, you can customize your data in various formats, such as tables, vertical bar graphs, and maps. This allows you to easily compare your data side by side and identify patterns and relationships that may not be apparent at first glance.

The dashboards in Kibana support several types of panels that you can use to display your data. Whether you want to create a bar chart, a pie chart, or a heatmap and bring all of them together in a customized view, creating a customized dashboard is the way to go!

Let's see in detail how this can be done:

1. First, we need to finalize the visualizations you need to use, or create the visualizations if not already created.

    As we are aware, a dashboard is created from visualizations; hence, the first step will involve creating them or ensuring that we have all the required representations saved in the library for the use case you are targeting.

    For example, we can create a visualization by clicking the **Create dashboard** button on the main dashboard page, as follows:

Figure 8.7 – The navigation to create a dashboard

2. The next step offers us two options to add visualizations. We can either create one or add one from the saved library by clicking the respective options, as shown here:

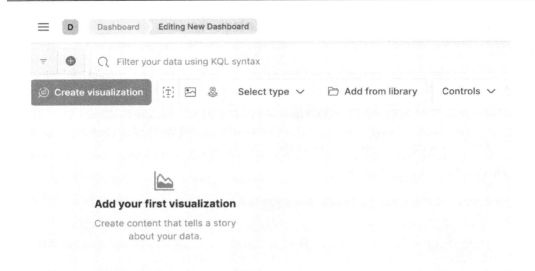

Figure 8.8 – The navigation to create a visualization or add one from the library

3. Next, if we click the **Create visualization** option, it will navigate us to the Lens tool, which we learned about in an earlier chapter. We can create the intended visualization here and click on **Save and return**, as shown in the following screenshot:

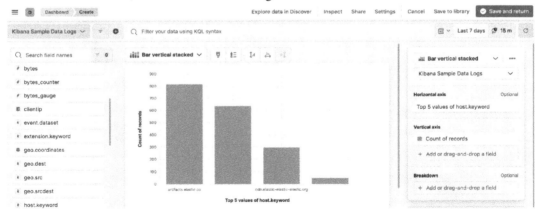

Figure 8.9 – Navigation to Lens via the Create dashboard page

4. Once done, we can now view the created Lens visualization added to the dashboard. We can add all the remaining visualizations similarly, and once done, clicking the **Save** button in the top-right corner of the page will help save the dashboard to the Kibana library.

The following screenshot depicts the result of the process:

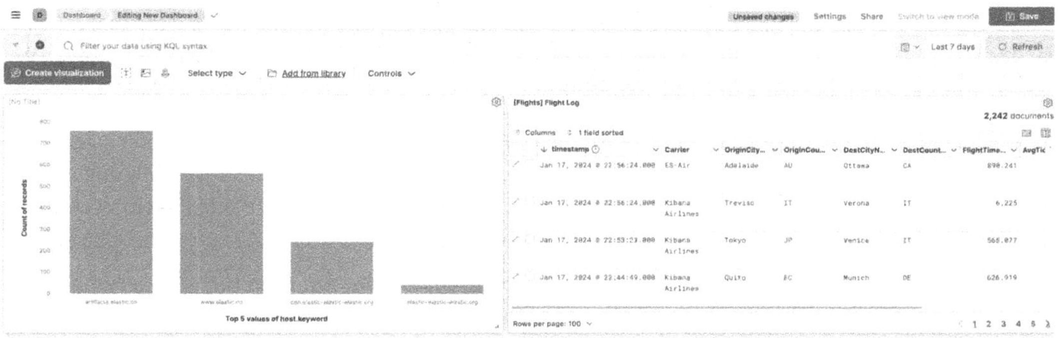

Figure 8.10 – The final result of the dashboard

In this section, we saw the step-by-step process to create a dashboard from start to finish.

Understanding a logging use case on a dashboard

In the heart of our bustling e-commerce platform, logs hum like a hidden orchestra, each line a cryptic note revealing the symphony of customer clicks and server whirs. These whispers of data, once scattered and silent, find their voice on a Kibana dashboard, transformed into vibrant visualizations that guide our decisions and safeguard our customers' journeys. For example, a bar chart can depict login attempts, and its bars could spike during weekend flash sales, a testament to our platform's resilience. Meanwhile, a heatmap could paint a geographical landscape of API calls, pinpointing regions experiencing sudden surges, prompting us to proactively scale resources. Every error message, once a frustrating riddle, could now be color-coded and categorized, allowing our support team to swiftly diagnose and resolve issues, ensuring seamless customer experiences.

Beyond troubleshooting, our Kibana dashboard becomes a crystal ball, predicting potential bottlenecks before they materialize. A line graph tracks memory usage, its gentle incline hinting at a server nearing its limit. With a click, we can drill down to specific microservices, identify resource hogs, and proactively scale or optimize, preventing outages before they can disrupt the shopping spree.

But the true magic lies in the stories woven from these digital threads. We can peer into log entries, witnessing a customer's triumphant purchase journey from hesitant search to satisfied checkout, a silent ode to our platform's effectiveness. Or we can trace the path of a fraudulent attempt, its serpentine trail exposing vulnerabilities, empowering us to tighten security measures and protect our customers' trust.

This Kibana dashboard, then, is more than just a data display; it's a window into the soul of our e-commerce ecosystem. It whispers insights, sings warnings, and dances with possibilities, transforming the cryptic language of logs into a symphony of knowledge, guiding us toward a future where every click resonates with success. Furthermore, let's learn more about logging use cases with a step-by-step process for an actual market use case in this next section of the logging adventure.

A logging adventure – from a stump to a Kibana symphony

Imagine traversing a dense forest of logs, each line a fallen branch whispering tales of your system's activity. Without a map, this journey can be daunting. Enter Kibana, your cartographer, ready to transform these whispers into a visual symphony:

1. **Act I – Setting the stage**: Our protagonist, the Elasticsearch index, stores the raw logs like scattered firewood. Kibana, the maestro, orchestrates the visualization. We begin by defining log stash pipelines, meticulously sifting through the logs, and extracting key fields such as timestamps, application names, and log levels. These fields become our instruments, ready to be played.

2. **Act II – The visual concerto**: With a flick of Kibana's baton, we summon the time series chart. Lines dance across the canvas, each depicting the frequency of different log levels over time. A sudden spike in errors? A dip in activity during server maintenance? These patterns become melodies, revealing the system's rhythm.

3. **Act III – Drilling down**: However, the concert holds deeper secrets. We zoom in with filters, focusing on specific applications or timeframes. The pie chart spins, showcasing the distribution of log levels for a chosen service. Is our e-commerce platform plagued by authentication failures? This visual aria exposes the culprit.

4. **Act IV – The grand finale**: The geolocation map paints the world with the system's footprint. Each log entry becomes a twinkling star, pinpointing the origin of the activity. Are users in Sydney experiencing more login issues than those in Melbourne? This spatial harmony exposes regional trends.

5. **Encore – Beyond the stage**: Kibana's magic extends beyond mere visuals. Alerts act as vigilant watchtowers, sounding alarms when predetermined thresholds are crossed. Dashboards become personalized command centers, housing a curated collection of visualizations for specific use cases.

6. **Curtain call – A symphony complete**: From raw logs to insightful melodies, Kibana transforms the logging landscape through the dashboard. With each visualization, we gain a deeper understanding of our system's health, performance, and user behavior. And so, the logging adventure concludes not with a whimper but with a joyous symphony, composed of data and conducted by the maestro, Kibana.

We're still learning the very basics, and we will now move on and dive into learning how the dashboard offers much more than just a set of few visualizations on the table.

Deep-diving into Kibana dashboards – where insights take center stage

Imagine a bustling marketplace, each stall overflowing with vibrant data insights. That's the essence of a Kibana dashboard – a curated space where key metrics and visualizations dance together, telling the story of your system.

Gone are the days of sifting through endless logs. Dashboards hand-pick the most critical information, presenting it in a clear, concise, and visually compelling way. Think of them as personalized newsfeeds, displaying only the data that matters most to you. But dashboards aren't just static snapshots. They're living, breathing entities. Filters and time ranges let you explore different perspectives, drilling down into specific details or zooming out to see the bigger picture. Like a magnifying glass, they focus your attention on anomalies, trends, and patterns that might otherwise go unnoticed.

And what's a marketplace without variety? Kibana has a smorgasbord of visualization types. Line charts track trends over time, pie charts slice and dice data by categories, and maps pinpoint activity across geographical locations. Each visualization plays a distinct role in the symphony of insights. But dashboards are more than just the sum of their parts. They're about storytelling, about weaving data into a narrative that informs decisions and drives action. By combining the right visualizations with thoughtful layouts and annotations, you can guide users through the data, revealing hidden truths and sparking new ideas.

So, next time you're lost in a sea of data, remember the power of Kibana dashboards. They're not just dashboards; they're data concierges, ready to lead you on a journey of discovery. Next up is the most important part, where we learn about sharing these insights with the world through the various share options available in the dashboard interface.

Sharing the dashboard

Kibana offers a variety of ways to share your saved searches, dashboards, Visualize Library visualizations, and Canvas workpads. To access these options, simply navigate to the **Share** menu in the toolbar. From there, you can choose from several sharing options that are available to you, as shown in the following screenshot:

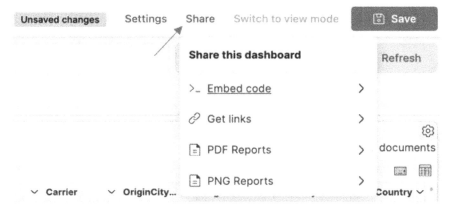

Figure 8.11 – The Share option on the dashboard

When we click the **Share** option, it gives us two ways to report and other ways to share the dashboard. When we see the reporting side of it, we can generate a PDF report, as shown here:

Figure 8.12 – The PDF Reports option on the dashboard

Upon clicking the **Generate PDF** option, it will simply download the dashboard on the local system as a PDF file. If optimized for printing, it will ensure to print all the pages in A4 size, which makes the viewing of the dashboard easier.

Alternatively, for users who intend to report the dashboard in the form of a PNG file, they can select the **PNG Reports** option, as shown in the following screenshot:

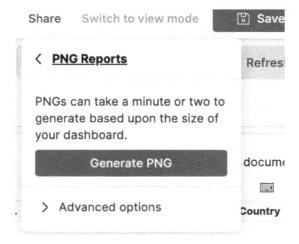

Figure 8.13 – The PNG Reports option on the dashboard

Furthermore, to avail yourself of the **Share** feature, you can share the dashboard in two ways – as a permalink or through an embedded code.

The permalink will generate a unique HTTP link that redirects users to the dashboard upon clicking; conversely, embedded code will enable the user to integrate the dashboard in their websites or frontend apps by leveraging the HTML code that the **Share** button generates. *Figure 8.14* shows that the link and the embedded code can then be generated in two ways, depending on the need of the hour:

- **Snapshot**: One useful feature of Kibana is the ability to share the current state of a dashboard through a snapshot URL. This URL encodes the current layout and configuration settings of the dashboard, allowing others to view it exactly as it is at that moment. However, it's important to note that any further edits or changes made to the dashboard will not be reflected in the snapshot URL. It is very similar to a screenshot that depicts the "frozen" state of a particular moment when it was taken.

- **Saved object**: In contrast, **Saved object** represents the last saved status of the dashboard. When a user saves their changes to a dashboard, it becomes a saved object, capturing all modifications made up to that point. This ensures that the dashboard can be accessed and viewed in its most recent state by anyone with the appropriate permissions.

Both the **Snapshot** and **Saved object** options serve different purposes when it comes to sharing dashboards in Kibana. While snapshots are ideal for sharing a specific version or snapshot of a dashboard's current state, **Saved object** provides access to the most up-to-date version of the dashboard.

Whether you choose to share a snapshot URL or access a saved object, Kibana offers flexibility and convenience in collaborating and disseminating information through its powerful visualization capabilities.

Let's say that we wish to share embedded code in the form of a snapshot; we can select the **Snapshot** option, as shown in the following screenshot:

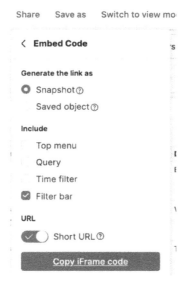

Figure 8.14 – The Embed Code option of the Share feature

And the sample `iframe` code to embed (i.e., the HTML code) appears like this:

```
<iframe src="https://juxwycstgeesmshyp-xxxxxxxxxxx.rp.strigo.io/
app/r/s/xAwTf" height="600" width="800"></iframe>
```

If we select the **Get links** (also known as the permalink) option to generate a saved object of the **Share** option feature, we can create a link similar to the following:

```
https://<link to the kibana dashboard>
```

Finally, you also have the option to generate JSON files for the Canvas workpad. To begin, access the Kibana home page and click on **Canvas**, as shown here:

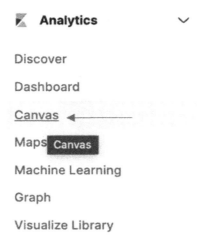

Figure 8.15 – The navigation to Canvas on the Kibana main menu

This will take you to an area where you can design and customize your workpads. Once you have created the desired workpad, you may want to share it with others for collaboration or reference purposes.

To share a workpad, open the specific one you wish to share from your list of existing workpads. Once opened, locate the toolbar at the top of the screen and click on **Share**, as shown here:

Figure 8.16 – The Share option in Canvas

A drop-down menu will appear, and from there, select **Download as JSON**, as shown here:

Figure 8.17 – The navigation to Download as JSON in Canvas

By downloading the workpad as a JSON file, you are able to easily distribute it among team members or store it for future use. This format ensures that all the visualizations and configurations within your workpad are preserved. Also, storing Kibana dashboards as a JSON file in Git repositories unleashes a universe of possibilities. Version control lets you track dashboard evolution, allowing easy rollbacks and comparisons. Collaboration flourishes as teams share and iterate on dashboards seamlessly. Plus, deployment becomes a breeze, with automated scripts pulling the latest JSON file for instant visualization magic.

By utilizing the Kibana dashboard and leveraging its sharing capabilities through JSON files, you can effectively communicate your data insights with others in a seamless manner. Whether it's for collaboration or archiving purposes, this functionality enhances the value and accessibility of your workpads.

In summary, these reports can include saved searches, visualizations, dashboards and Canvas workpads. Moreover, another option is **CSV Download**, which allows you to generate and download CSV files of your saved searches. This is particularly useful if you want to analyze data in a spreadsheet format or share it with others who prefer working with CSV files. The PNG reports that you saw earlier enable you to generate and download PNG files of your saved objects. It's worth noting that this feature and the PDF report are only available with a subscription. These sharing options offered by Kibana give you the flexibility to collaborate with others or present your findings in different formats. Whether it's downloading CSV files for further analysis, generating visual reports in the PNG or PDF formats, or sharing dashboards in the form of a saved object or snapshot, Kibana has got you covered.

Moreover, the **Share** dashboard feature empowers you to automate corporate report generation, freeing you from manual data wrangling. Imagine setting up a scheduled task that automatically captures your insightful dashboards weekly or monthly. This dynamic snapshot gets exported as a PDF or PNG file, ready to be seamlessly integrated into your management reports. CxOs receive fresh, data-driven insights on a regular basis, keeping them informed and engaged. So, we can refrain from manual updates or last-minute scrambles because Kibana's **Share** feature ensures our reports are always up to date and visually captivating, leaving a lasting impression on key stakeholders.

Summary

In this chapter, we studied in detail how a dashboard can enable users to see data insights all on one page, and we saw how to leverage features such as query and filter reflecting on every visualization present on the dashboard.

We also learned how we can either begin by exploring sample dashboards or create our own dashboard from scratch, adding all the use case-specific visualizations with diverse representation styles. Finally, we explored how we can start sharing these very interesting dashboards with team members, peers, or customers, presenting them with the insights that we have successfully extracted from a dataset.

In the next chapter, we shall go through some advanced concepts such as scripted fields, which will enable us to target a specific use case.

Part 4:
Querying on Kibana and Advanced Concepts

In this last part, we will dive deeper into data's depths to see where Kibana transforms from a visualization hub to a data manipulation maestro. We'll wield the expressive **Elasticsearch Query Language (ES|QL)**, crafting bespoke queries that sculpt insights with surgical precision. Query DSL joins the party, revealing its powerful constructs for complex data wrangling. But wait, there's more! Kibana's runtime fields step into the spotlight, dynamically generating data points on the fly for deeper analysis. Finally, we'll unlock the secrets of advanced Kibana settings, fine-tuning dashboards for maximum visual impact and intuitive exploration. Prepare to push Kibana's boundaries and unleash its hidden potential – data whispers, and it's time we listen with razor-sharp precision.

This part has the following chapters:

- *Chapter 9, ES|QL and Advanced Kibana Concepts*
- *Chapter 10, Query DSL and Management through Kibana*

9

ES|QL and Advanced Kibana Concepts

Elasticsearch Query Language (**ES|QL**) stands at the forefront of Elasticsearch 8.11, offering a powerful and intuitive means to interact with and extract valuable insights from your data. This query language is designed to provide users with a flexible and expressive way to formulate complex queries and searches. With ES|QL, users can seamlessly navigate and explore their Elasticsearch indices, harnessing their capabilities to filter, aggregate, and sort data efficiently. The latest version introduces enhancements to the query language, emphasizing its role in simplifying the querying process while maintaining the scalability and speed that Elasticsearch is renowned for.

Whether you are a seasoned Elasticsearch user or a newcomer, ES|QL's user-friendly syntax and advanced features empower you to delve into your data with precision, making it a cornerstone of efficient data exploration and analysis.

It is time to take a deep dive into how the query language is built and functions from the ground up. We will cover the following topics in this chapter:

- Learning the ES|QL building blocks

- Understanding how ES|QL works

- Exploring advanced Kibana concepts

Technical requirements

As per the basic requirements, we assume that you have data ingested in the cluster and that Elasticsearch and Kibana are set up on the nodes of (any) environment (the cloud or locally).

Once Kibana is up and running, we can navigate to **Kibana | Try sample data**, select **Other sample datasets**, click on the **Add data for Kibana_sample_data_ecommerce** dataset, and then **Kibana_sample_data_logs**.

Learning the ES|QL building blocks

ES|QL is built upon a foundation of robust query capabilities and an intuitive syntax that empowers users to interact effectively with Elasticsearch data. At its core, ES|QL leverages the Elasticsearch query **DSL** (short for **Domain-Specific Language**), providing a comprehensive set of commands to articulate complex queries. The language is designed for flexibility, allowing users to seamlessly navigate the intricate structure of Elasticsearch indices.

ES|QL's architecture incorporates a deep understanding of Elasticsearch's distributed nature, ensuring optimal performance across large-scale datasets. It embraces principles of scalability, enabling users to harness its capabilities in diverse and demanding environments. The development of ES|QL involves a collaborative effort from the Elasticsearch community, with continuous enhancements and updates being introduced to adapt to evolving user needs and accommodate the latest features of Elasticsearch. Its building blocks prioritize simplicity and clarity, making it accessible to both seasoned Elasticsearch users and those new to the platform.

The ES|QL syntax has been crafted with specific objectives in mind:

- Enabling the iterative exploration of Elasticsearch datasets, allowing users to initiate a basic document query and progressively refine it through incremental steps. Refinement is most conveniently achieved by appending additional instructions at the end and on the right-hand side of the query.

- Providing users with the capability to specify the desired outcome of a query without necessitating an in-depth understanding of the intricacies of query execution.

- Catering to users familiar with SQL, SPL, or analogous languages, such as Kusto, ensuring a seamless transition and ease of use for those with existing language proficiencies.

Furthermore, ES|QL adheres to the following fundamental principles:

- The language's basic components are commands linked through Unix-like pipes, allowing users to easily enhance and refine existing queries.

- While it is preferable to avoid hints for optimizing query execution, there might be instances where such hints are necessary to enable specific optimizations.

- Commands maintain semantic independence; only inputted data and command arguments influence the output. The semantics of a command should not be affected by preceding or subsequent commands.

- The data structure upon which commands operate adheres to a tabular format, and the output generated by an ES|QL query can be presented in a tabular structure as well.

To understand how commands in the query language are structured, the key points to take into consideration are the following:

- A command initiates with a command name followed by whitespace and command names, and keywords are case-sensitive.

- Command names and keywords adhere to the *[a-z][a-z0-9](-[a-z][a-z0-9])** pattern in kebab-case.

- As much as possible, command arguments should be specified using the defined syntax building blocks (e.g., scalar expressions and literals). Avoid using syntactical elements exclusively employed in one or a few commands.

- Command names typically describe the logical transformations applied to incoming data rather than specifying the content, shape of the result, or implementation specifics. For example, use `sort` instead of `sorted` or `quicksort`.

It is essential to point out here that ES|QL operates without the need for translation or transpositions to Query DSL. Instead, every query undergoes a meticulous breakdown, with an initial interpretation to discern its intended meaning, followed by thorough validation for accuracy. Subsequently, each query is optimized for optimal performance. A systematic process is then established for the execution of the query across diverse nodes within a cluster. The designated target nodes adeptly manage the query, dynamically adjusting the execution plan on the fly by leveraging the framework provided by ES|QL. The outcome is the generation of remarkably swift queries as a default feature. For a tangible example, you can refer to the nightly benchmarks link at `https://elasticsearch-benchmarks.elastic.co/#tracks/esql/nightly/default/30d` for a comprehensive comparison, showcasing the efficiency and speed achieved through ES|QL's unique approach to query execution.

In this section, we've seen that ES|QL's design makes things work smarter, not harder. By reusing query results, it eliminates wasteful computations and the need for tangled code, ultimately saving you valuable time and resources. We can safely say that it is not just an API but also a simple and powerful way to transform your approach to searching. Now, let's move on to understand how it works.

Understanding how ES|QL works

The query language works fundamentally through a source command, and it can be followed by (optional) commands called **processing commands**. They are separated by a pipe (|); hence, ES|QL is also referred to as Elastic's **piped query language**. The source command results into a table formation from the data in Elasticsearch, as shown in the following figure:

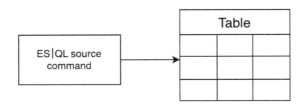

Figure 9.1 – The source command concept in Elasticsearch

Three different source commands that are supported, which are FROM, ROW, and SHOW.

Here's a simple example of how ES|QL works. Imagine you have an index named products that contains product data, and you want to find all products with a price above $50.

With ES|QL, you could write the following query:

```
FROM products WHERE price > 50;
```

This query looks just like a standard SQL query, but ES|QL translates it into Elasticsearch's query language, retrieving the desired results. Refer to the following figure:

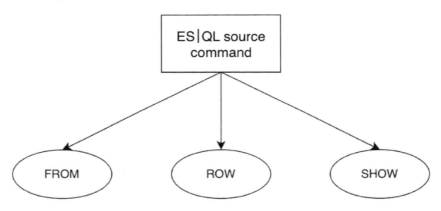

Figure 9.2 – The three source commands in Elasticsearch

From the preceding figure, we can see the following:

- FROM results in each row signifying a document, while each column corresponds to a specific field, accessible by its respective field name.

- ROW generates a table containing data retrieved from a data stream, index, or alias. In the resulting table, every row represents a document, and each column corresponds to a field, accessible by its designated field name.

- SHOW provides details regarding the deployment to obtain information on its version, hash, and date of build.

The processing commands thereafter will result in another table changing/transforming into an updated number of rows and/or columns, as shown in the following diagram:

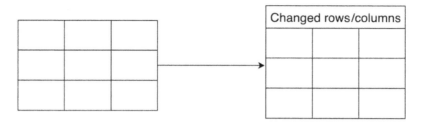

Figure 9.3 – The three source commands in Elasticsearch

There are multiple processing commands that can be used, and they can be listed as shown in the following diagram:

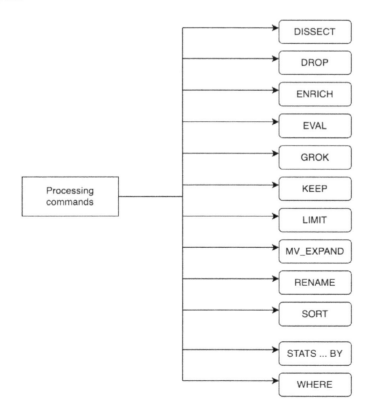

Figure 9.4 – The processing commands in Elasticsearch

As per the preceding diagram, each of these functions can be summarized as follows:

- DISSECT: This excels at structured data. It efficiently extracts specific parts of a string as columns, based on a defined delimiter pattern. This makes it ideal for processing data with a consistent, repetitive format. Conversely, GROK handles diverse patterns, where it leverages the flexibility of regular expressions to match complex patterns and extract varied data elements. However, this power comes with potential performance overhead. The important point here is to choose the right tool for the job. Opt for DISSECT when working with well-structured, repetitive data for speed and efficiency, and select GROK when facing diverse or unpredictable data structures, or when intricate pattern matching is required.

  Here is the DISSECT syntax:

  ```
  DISSECT input "pattern" [APPEND_SEPARATOR="   <    separator>"]
  ```

  Where Input is the column holding the string that you aim to organize. If the column comprises of multiple values, DISSECT will handle each of them individually.

- DROP: This surgically removes columns from datasets, enabling you to focus on the most pertinent information and reduce unnecessary clutter.

  Here is the syntax:

  ```
  DROP columns
  ```

- ENRICH: This allows you to augment your dataset by incorporating data from existing indices as additional columns, by applying an enrich policy. Note that ENRICH takes place at search time instead of the usual indexing time, with the performance of the cluster taken into consideration.

  Here is the syntax:

  ```
  ENRICH policy [ON match_field] [WITH [new_name1 = ]field1, [new_
  name2 = ]field2, ...]
  ```

  Imagine ENRICH as a data Cupid, wielding the match_field arrow to pinpoint perfect record pairings from the enrich index. These connections breathe life into your data, weaving enriching threads within your landscape. When Cupid takes a break, ENRICH smartly relies on matching column names, effortlessly streamlining integration and saving you precious time for deeper analysis. So, let ENRICH's matchmaking magic elevate your data to its most meaningful form.

- EVAL: This command transforms your datasets into dynamic playgrounds, enabling you to create insightful new columns using a diverse arsenal of functions. Dance with aggregates such as avg, min, and max to uncover patterns and trends, or explore the mathematical realm with abs, SIN, TAN, and so on.

  Here is the syntax:

  ```
  EVAL column1 = value1[, ..., columnN = valueN]
  ```

In this syntax, `column` and `value` stand for the column name and column value, respectively.

For example, consider the following:

```
FROM company
  | SORT id_no
  | KEEP phone_number, address, distance
  | EVAL distance_meter= distance* 1000, distance_cm = height *
10000
```

Here, `phone_number`, `address`, and `distance` are the column names, and `distance_meter` and `distance_cm` are the calculated column names, added using the EVAL function. The pipe is used to concatenate all the arguments to form the query.

- GROK: This is very similar to `DISSECT` and helps you to process unstructured data into a structured format. It identifies a string based on a pattern rooted in regular expressions and extracts designated keys, renaming them as specific columns.

  Here is the syntax:

  ```
  GROK input "pattern"
  ```

  Here, `pattern` is the GROK pattern, which uses regular expressions.

  Although GROK works very similar to `DISSECT`, it uses regular expressions, whereas `DISSECT` works by breaking up a string using a delimiter-based pattern.

- KEEP: This lets you create a personalized playlist of columns, deciding exactly which ones make the cut and in what order they appear. It's like curating the perfect mixtape for your data analysis, ensuring you have the most relevant information at your fingertips, arranged in a way that makes sense to you.

  Here is the syntax:

  ```
  KEEP columns
  ```

  Here, `columns` act as a parameter, which can be used to name the columns in the data. If there is a case where you don't know the exact name of the columns, then you can also use a wildcard, such as the following:

  ```
  FROM company
  | keep g*
  ```

  Here, `company` is the column name and the columns that needs to be kept in the result. Here, that column starts with `g`, as per the query example from earlier.

- LIMIT: This allows you to restrict the quantity of returned rows in the result of the query. However, the maximum rows that queries can return is 10,000. The default for LIMIT is 10 in the standard DSL.

Here is the syntax:

```
LIMIT max_number_of_rows
```

Here's an example:

```
FROM company
| LIMIT 5
where we are limiting the rows to be 5 in the result of the
query.
```

- MV_EXPAND: This transforms columns with multiple values into individual rows for each value, while it creates same/duplicate values for the other columns in the table.

  Here is the syntax:

  ```
  MV_EXPAND column
  ```

- RENAME: This, as the name describes, simply renames the columns as required. If the name to be renamed already exists, then it is replaced by the new name given in the query.

  Here is the syntax:

  ```
  RENAME old_name1 AS new_name1[, ..., old_nameN   AS new_nameN]
  ```

  Here, old_name1,2,..X is the older name that needs to be renamed, and new_name1,2,..X is the new name that we wish to give the column name.

- SORT: The SORT command takes the aforementioned one or more columns into consideration in order to sort the table. The default sort order is ASC, but we can change it to DESC by adding that to the query.

  Here is the syntax:

  ```
  SORT columnX [ASC/DESC] [NULLS FIRST/NULLS LAST]
  ```

  Here, columnX can be column1, column2, and so on.

- STATS...BY: This allows users to bring rows together based on their shared values and then calling out for stats, such as AVG, MAX, MIN, and MEDIAN, to summarize each group's strengths and weaknesses. It's like having a personal sports analyst for your data, revealing key insights about each group's performance and helping you make informed decisions.

  Here is the syntax:

  ```
  STATS [col1 =] expression1[, ..., [colN =]   expressionN] [BY
  grouping_col1[, ..., grouping_colN]]
  ```

  Here, colX is the aggregated column value's name, which, if omitted, will see the value replaced by the respective expressionX.

- WHERE: This is the command that enables you to add a condition, which, if true, includes all the respective rows in the result table.

Here is the syntax:

```
FROM employees
  | KEEP address, phone_number, distance
  | WHERE LENGTH (address) < 15
```

Here, `phone_number`, `address`, and `distance` are the column names, and the `WHERE` condition, if true, will enable the query to get all the rows that have an address length below `15` letters.

In this section, we studied how ES|QL is built and the foundational concepts on which it works. The implementations of the query language can depend on the use case requirements and combine many of the different commands we've learned so far.

Let's take a real market example of ES|QL implementation – fueling a live sports game. The step-by-step implementation process is as follows:

1. **Data ingestion**: Use data pipelines such as Logstash/Beats or Elastic Agent to capture live sports data feeds from APIs, web scraping, or real-time event streams.

   This data could include play-by-play updates, scores, player stats, team information, and fan sentiment.

2. **Index design**: Create dedicated data views for different datasets (e.g., games, plays, players, and teams). Define mappings for each index with relevant fields, such as `timestamp`, team, `player`, `score`, and `event type`.

   Optimize indexing for fast retrieval based on frequent queries, such as real-time game scores or player performance during a specific timeframe.

3. **ES|QL queries for live updates**: Use ES|QL queries to fetch real-time data based on various criteria, such as the following:

```
Current score:
FROM games
  | KEEP team, scores
  | WHERE game_id == "live";
Player stats:
FROM players
  | KEEP players, points, rebounds, assists
  | WHERE team LIKE "HOME" AND game_id == "live";
Team standings:
FROM teams
  | KEEP team, wins, losses
  | SORT wins DESC;
```

4. **Visualizations and dashboards**: You can integrate ES|QL with data visualization tools to create live dashboards, displaying real-time scoreboards with dynamic updates and showing player performance charts and shot maps. Moreover, you can visualize team possession and scoring trends throughout the game.

5. **Fan engagement and alerts**: Use ES|QL to power interactive features and fan engagement; enable fans to search for specific plays or player stats in real time. You can also set up alerts for favorite teams' scoring updates or close game situations.

Additionally, you can personalize recommendations for content based on individual fan preferences.

ES|QL bridges the gap between familiar SQL syntax and the powerful world of Elasticsearch data. Imagine ES|QL as a translator, turning SQL queries you already know into Elasticsearch commands that unlock insights hidden within your data. Instead of tables and rows, ES|QL operates on Elasticsearch indices and documents. Documents, flexible data structures holding various information, become your canvas. You can filter, aggregate, and join these documents using familiar SQL clauses, such as WHERE, GROUP BY, and JOIN, adapted to handle Elasticsearch nuances.

Think of aggregations as powerful paintbrushes. They let you summarize and manipulate your data, calculating averages, counts, and even custom metrics. ES|QL empowers you to explore facets of your data that you might miss with simple searches.

However, ESQL's magic goes beyond basic SQL. It leverages Elasticsearch's full potential with specialized functions, such as geospatial queries, time-series analysis, and even machine learning tasks. You can analyze location data, track trends over time, and even predict future values, all within the comfort of familiar SQL syntax. ES|QL simplifies complex data exploration, letting you focus on extracting insights, not wrestling with Elasticsearch intricacies. It's like having a superpower to unlock the hidden stories within your Elasticsearch data, using the language you already know.

By implementing ESQL, developers can create dynamic and engaging live sports experiences, keeping fans on the edge of their seats and providing valuable insights into a game's real-time flow.

Remember, ES|QL is still evolving, but it's already a game-changer for anyone familiar with SQL who wants to tap into the vast potential of Elasticsearch. So, pick up your ES|QL brush and start painting your data masterpiece!

Next, let us move on to understanding the different kinds of advanced concepts, such as runtime fields, that we can implement in Kibana.

Advanced Kibana concepts

Kibana has several implementations that are designed for very specific use case requirements, and runtime fields is one of them. Let's explore and understand them.

Runtime fields

Forget static schemas; Elasticsearch runtime fields are your dynamic paintbrushes! They let you create fields on the fly, transforming your data on demand within your queries. Imagine a data sculptor, molding your documents with temporary fields based on your needs.

There's no need to re-index or restructure your data. Runtime fields are calculated at query time, pulling information from existing fields or even combining them into new ones. Think of it as a temporary data transformation, enriching your documents without changing their core structure. These dynamic fields are versatile. You can extract specific values using Grok patterns, calculate aggregates such as averages or counts, or even perform complex calculations. They're perfect for adding context, exploring data from different angles, and tailoring your results to your specific needs.

And the best part? Runtime fields are invisible in your source data, keeping your original documents clean. They're like temporary tools, leaving no trace after they've shaped your query results.

These fields in Kibana serve as a powerful feature that allows users to derive new insights and manipulate data within their Elasticsearch indices. They enable the creation of dynamic and custom fields on the fly by applying scripted expressions to existing data during query time, where they can be constructed using either Painless, a secure scripting language, or other supported scripting languages. This flexibility empowers users to perform complex calculations, transform data, and generate visualizations tailored to their specific analytical needs. They play a pivotal role in enhancing the agility and versatility of data analysis within Kibana, offering a dynamic way to interact with and interpret Elasticsearch data. Runtime fields were earlier known as *scripted fields* until the term was deprecated in the recent versions of Kibana. So, let's start to unleash your creativity! Let's use these runtime fields to filter data based on unseen patterns, build custom metrics on the fly, and even combine data from different sources. They're your key to unlocking hidden insights and crafting the perfect data canvas for your Elasticsearch queries.

Let's look at a step-by-step guide to create a runtime field in Kibana:

1.   Navigate to the Kibana main menu and click on **Stack Management**:

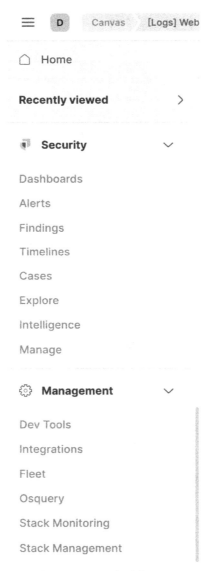

Figure 9.5 – Navigating to the Kibana main menu

Alternatively, we can also navigate to **Discover**, click on the **Data views** dropdown, and select **Add field to this data view**, as displayed in the following figure:

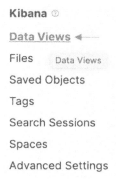

Figure 9.6 – The Kibana Discover option to create a new runtime field

2.   If we choose to go through Stack Management to create a runtime field, then navigate to **Stack Management | Data Views**, as shown in the following screenshot:

Figure 9.7 – Navigating to Data Views in Stack Management in Kibana

3.   Select the data view you wish to add the runtime field to, and then click **Add field**.

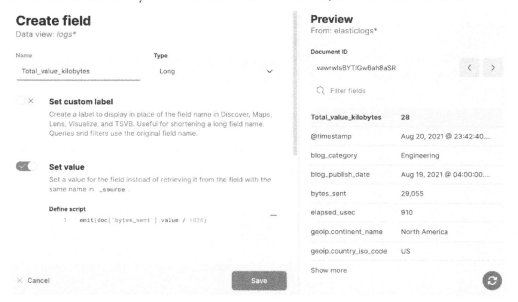

Figure 9.8 – The Add field button on the Data Views page

4. Enter the desired field name, and choose the appropriate type.

    Select **Set value** and create the script, ensuring alignment with the chosen type to prevent issues across applications utilizing the data view. Add a Painless script if the runtime field needs code to be implemented to fetch values in the respective documents of the data view, as shown here:

Figure 9.9 – The creation of a runtime field

In the preceding example, we added a new field named `Total_value_kilobytes` with a **Long** type, and we added a script in the **Set value** section. For assistance in defining the script, make use of the preview feature, which will validate the definition. It is a great way to confirm the script is good to go before we add a field to our data view. You can also filter the fields list by entering keywords in the **Filter fields** option. Finally, click **Save** to create the field, and you're done!

5. Proceed to **Discover** in Kibana, and select the appropriate data view and time picker to confirm the successful creation of the runtime field, as shown in the following screenshot:

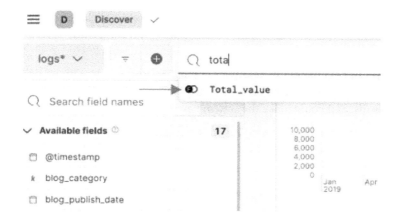

Figure 9.10 – Verification of the created runtime field in Discover

6. You can also find the field in the search bar to start implementing the KQL/Lucene queries on the same field or filters can be used too to find the field, as shown here:

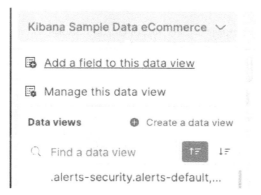

Figure 9.11 – Navigating to display a runtime field to use it in query languages

While runtime fields in Kibana offer flexibility and on-the-fly customization, they come with certain drawbacks that users should consider:

- **Performance impact**: The dynamic nature of runtime fields means that they are calculated at query time. This on-the-fly computation can lead to increased query execution times, potentially impacting overall performance, especially when dealing with large datasets.

- **Limited index optimization**: Runtime fields are created and computed during query execution rather than being precomputed and indexed. This can result in a lack of optimization compared to fields defined during index mapping, potentially affecting search efficiency.

- **Resource consumption**: The real-time computation of runtime fields can consume additional computational resources, particularly when dealing with complex scripts or large datasets. This may lead to increased server load and resource utilization.

- **Complexity and maintenance**: Managing and maintaining many runtime fields can introduce complexity to the system. Users should be cautious about creating an excessive number of runtime fields, as it could make the system harder to manage and understand.

- **Security considerations**: Depending on the scripting language used, runtime fields can introduce security considerations. Users should be mindful of potential security risks associated with the scripting language employed for these dynamic fields.

It's essential for users to carefully weigh the advantages of runtime fields against these drawbacks, considering their specific use case, dataset size, and performance requirements. In some scenarios, predefining fields during index mapping might be a more efficient and optimized approach. Let's move on to understanding and implementing the few advanced settings that we have as a part of Kibana's admin settings.

Advanced Kibana settings

Advanced Kibana settings encompass a spectrum of configurations and options that go beyond the standard settings accessible through the user interface. These settings delve into the intricacies of Kibana's behavior, allowing users to fine-tune and optimize the platform to meet specific requirements. Ranging from performance enhancements to customizing visualizations and handling security measures, advanced Kibana settings provide users with a comprehensive toolkit for tailoring the platform to their unique needs. Navigating these advanced configurations requires a nuanced understanding of Kibana's architecture and functionality, enabling users to unlock the full potential of the platform and tailor it to their specific use cases. When you navigate to the Kibana main menu and click **Stack management | Advanced settings**, there are various settings that you can select and modify. A few examples of the most used advanced settings are as follows:

- `csv:separator`: The default is `,`. This is used to define the separator string for exported values.

- `autocomplete:useTimeRange`: The default is turned on. When this is turned off, your dataset will be responsible for indicating the suggestions instead of the time range.

- `csv:quoteValuesc`: The default is turned on. Enable this property to enclose exported values in quotes.

- `DateFormat`: This specifies the format for displaying well-formatted dates.

- `dateFormat:dowc`: The default is *MMM D, YYYY @ HH:mm:ss.SSS*. This is used to determine the starting day of the week.

- `dateFormat:scaled`: The default is **Sunday**. This creates a flexible format for timestamps in time-based data. The format adjusts automatically based on the spacing between measurements, using standard `ISO8601` intervals as guidelines.

- `bfetch:disableCompression`: The default is enabled. Turning this off makes debugging individual requests easier, but responses will be `bigger if DefaultIndex : Default` is null.

  If there is no index set by the user, then the index mentioned as default will be used as the index to start ingesting the data.

- `dateFormat:tz`: The default is set to pick up the browser's format. This essentially sets the time zone used by Kibana.

- `DefaultRoute`: The default is set to `/app/home`. This setting customizes Kibana spaces to greet users with the most relevant views. Set a default landing page for each space to streamline their experience.

- `fields:popularLimit`: The default is set to 10. This setting sets the limit for displaying the most popular fields out of the top N.

- `fileUpload:maxFileSize`: The default is set to 100 MB, but the maximum is 1 GB. This setting is responsible for defining the size number when a user tries to import files to a cluster.

- `DateNanosFormat`: The default is set to *MMM D, YYYY @ HH:mm:ss.SSSSSSSSS*. Users can tailor the display of dates in the Elasticsearch `date_nanos` format to their exact preferences, ensuring clarity and consistency in their data.

- `filterEditor:suggestValues`: The default is *enabled*. If you disable this, then it will not allow the KQL to autocomplete, and it will not suggest values for the field upon typing in it.

- `format:bytes:defaultPattern`: The default is `0,0.[0]b`. This allows a user to specify the default numeral pattern format for the bytes format.

- `filters:pinnedByDefault`: The default is *disabled*. Enabling this setting ensures that filters remain persistently pinned across various contexts, providing a cohesive filtering experience.

- `MetaFields`: The default is _source, _id, _index, and _score. Even fields residing outside the _source realm are gracefully incorporated into document visualizations within Kibana, ensuring a holistic perspective.

- `metrics:allowStringIndices`: The default is *disabled*. This enables the use of Elasticsearch indices in TSVB visualizations.

- `histogram:barTarget`: The default is *50*. The setting specifies the number of bars to generate when date histograms use the auto interval.

- `search:queryLanguage`: The default is *KQL*. The system empowers users to tailor their queries by offering a choice between KQL and Lucene syntax, ensuring adaptability and control over search strategies.

- `histogram:maxBars`: The default is *1,000*. This setting ensures optimized density in date and number histograms throughout Kibana by dynamically adjusting bucket intervals based on test queries, enhancing visual clarity and performance.

- `metrics:max_buckets` : The default is *2,000*. This setting impacts the TSVB histogram density, and it is recommended to be set higher than `histogram:maxBars`.

- `query:allowLeadingWildcards` : The default is enabled. This crucial setting controls the launchpad of your searches – the leading asterisk wildcard (*). Unleashing its power lets you match any character sequence, opening doors to expansive exploration but potentially taxing resources. Remember, like a culinary spice, wield this flexibility with care, balancing the thrill of discovery with smooth search performance.

- `savedObjects:perPage` : The default is *20*. The setting sets the number of objects to show on each page of the list of saved objects.

- `shortDots:enable`: The default is disabled. When enabled, it gracefully abbreviates lengthy field names, transforming `qaa.roo.pee` into the more compact `q.r.p` for a smoother visual experience.

- `sort:options`: The default is *disabled*. This setting provides options such as sort order (ASC/DSC) and sort mode (min/max) for the Elasticsearch `sort` parameter.

- `query:queryString:options`: The default is set to *true* with the following command:

  ```
  {"analyze_wildcard": true}
  ```

This setting grants you the ability to meticulously tailor how the Lucene query string parser interprets and processes search queries, ensuring precise and efficient results.

- `savedObjects:listingLimit`: The default is *1,000*. This setting determines how many saved objects are retrieved simultaneously when viewing their lists, ensuring efficient loading and optimal performance.

- `state:storeInSessionStorage`: The default is *disabled*. This feature is still being tested and might not be available in future versions. It's designed to help with long URLs, which can occur when Kibana saves a lot of information in a website address. Turning it on will store some of that information in your browser instead of the URL, making the address bar look less cluttered.

- `theme:darkMode`: The default is disabled. Switch to Kibana's dark theme for better nighttime viewing. Don't forget to refresh the browser link in which Kibana is running!

- `timepicker:quickRanges`: The default is the following:

  ```
  [{
  "from": "now/d",
  "to": "now/d",
  "display": "Today"
  },
  {
  "from": "now/w",
  ```

```
"to": "now/w",
"display": "This week"
},
{
"from": "now-15m",
"to": "now",
"display": "Last 15 minutes"
}]
```

Here's a rephrased version of the text, aiming for clarity and conciseness:

```
To customize the quick time ranges in the filter:
Create a list of time ranges, like a menu of options.
Each range should be structured as a mini profile, including:
"from": The starting point of the range (format it correctly).
"to": The ending point of the range (format it correctly too).
"display": The name you want to show for the range in the
filter.
```

- `timepicker:refreshIntervalDefaults`: The default is the following:

```
{
"pause": true,
"value": 60000
}
```

To set a default refresh rate for the time filter, imagine a clock that automatically updates to show the latest data. You can control how often it ticks by setting a default refresh interval and measuring the interval in milliseconds (thousandths of a second).

Here is an example:

`{"pause": true, "value": 12000}` refreshes every 12 seconds.

- `timepicker:timeDefaults`: The default is the following:

```
{
"from": "now-15m",
"to": "now"
}
```

To set a default time range for Kibana when it launches it is like setting a welcome message! Specify the time range you want Kibana to show by default when it's first opened.

- **Format it as a pair**: Create an object with two properties:

  - `from`: The starting point of the time range (format it correctly)

  - `to`: The ending point of the time range (format it correctly too)

- `truncate:maxHeight`: The default is `115`.

  This setting is used to control how much space table cells take up. You can set a maximum height or use `0` to show everything.

A key point to remember is that modifying advanced settings can impact stability and security. It is important to be careful when making changes cautiously, understand their consequences, and always back up your Kibana configuration before applying them.

Summary

In this chapter, we took a deep dive into ES|QL, Elasticsearch's query language, where we have explored its building blocks such as indices, mappings, and queries to understand how data is structured and retrieved. We also grasped the magic of near-real-time search, which lets us perform analysis on live streams such as sports updates or financial transactions. We saw how we can unlock the hidden potential of Kibana with advanced settings such as custom index patterns, time formatting, and security controls. By mastering these elements, you'll transform from a data consumer to a real-time data maestro, wielding ES|QL and Kibana to extract hidden patterns and insights from the ever-flowing stream of information.

Remember, advanced settings are powerful tools. However, it is important to use them wisely, backed up by understanding and caution. Well, with ES|QL and Kibana in hand, you're now ready to conquer the ever-changing world of real-time data, transforming insights into action! Next, we will explore another query language for the Kibana dev console, and we'll look at some interesting management implementations for Kibana.

10

Query DSL and Management through Kibana

Congratulations! You've reached the final frontier of your Kibana journey: mastering Query **Domain Specific Language** (**DSL**) and leveraging its power through the intuitive interface. Kibana's power lies in its ability to sift through mountains of data, and Query DSL acts as your magic shovel. This JSON-based language lets you craft precise queries, from simple keyword searches to intricate Boolean combinations. With Query DSL, Kibana transforms from a data viewer to a data interrogator, empowering you to uncover hidden insights and answer your toughest questions, line by insightful line.

In this closing chapter, we'll shed the training wheels and delve into the heart of data exploration. We'll unlock the secrets of Query DSL, crafting precise and nuanced search queries that pinpoint the exact information you crave. Then, we'll see how Kibana transforms Query DSL into a user-friendly playground, where building complex searches becomes a visual adventure.

Imagine crafting queries that dance across time and space, effortlessly filtering through oceans of data to unearth hidden gems. With Query DSL, this is your reality. We'll equip you with the knowledge to navigate its syntax, wield its operators like tools of discovery, and bend it to your will. But fear not, syntax samurai! Kibana stands beside you, translating your intent into visual constructs, ready to guide you through every step of the search-crafting process.

Let's start digging into the concepts of Query DSL and other management concepts in the following list:

- Learning Query DSL
- Deep-diving management concepts – **Role-Based Access Control** (**RBAC**)
- Exploring watchers

Technical requirements

As per the basic requirements, we assume that you have data ingested in the cluster and that Elasticsearch and Kibana are set up on the nodes of (any) environment (cloud or local).

Once Kibana is up and running, we can navigate to **Kibana** home page and click on **Try sample data | Other sample data sets**, and then click on the **Add data for Kibana_sample_data_ecommerce** dataset. We shall be using this dataset for creating the visualization on Lens in this chapter.

Learning about Query DSL

Query DSL, as we discussed earlier, is a JSON-based DSL that empowers you to construct intricate search queries on the data present in the Elasticsearch cluster. It's structured like an **abstract syntax tree (AST)** with two fundamental building blocks: leaf query clauses for pinpointing specific values within fields, and compound query clauses for orchestrating multiple queries using logical combinations or modifying their behavior. The context in which these clauses are used, either query or filter, significantly impacts their behavior. If we are to learn to write queries from scratch, we can investigate querying all the data in a particular index. For example, in MS SQL language, we say, `Select * from employees`, where `employees` is a table in the MS SQL database.

Here, in **Console**, we implement a similar logic to write a DSL query as follows:

```
GET kibana_sample_data_ecommerce/_search;
```

Here, `kibana_sample_data_ecommerce` is an index in Elasticsearch. This query will simply return all the documents present in this index on Elasticsearch in JSON format.

To run DSL queries, we would need to navigate Kibana by going to the **Kibana** main menu and clicking on **Stack management | Dev Tools | Console**.

When we navigate to **Console**, we get a screen with a pop-up that will have the reference to DSL queries. We can click on the **Dismiss** button (as shown in the following screenshot) to close the popup and start looking at queries we can execute in **Console**.

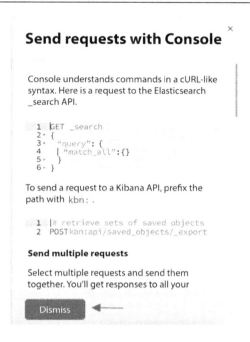

Figure 10.1 – A view of the first-time popup in Dev Tools

Console, as shown in the following screenshot, is a place to implement all the DSL queries to search, ingest, and process the data through simple, easy-to-write queries:

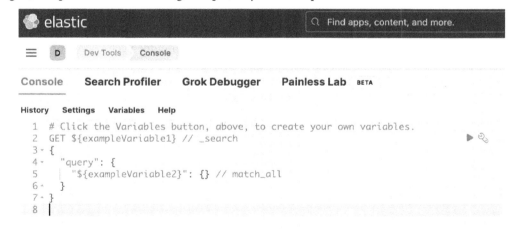

Figure 10.2 – A view of Console in Dev Tools in Kibana

The umbrella of Query DSL is divided into eight parts, as listed in the following figure:

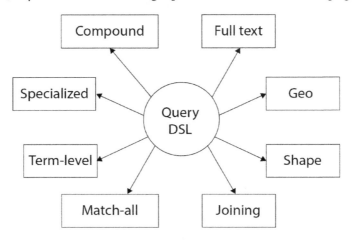

Figure 10.3 – The types of DSL queries in Elasticsearch

Let us learn about each of these in the following sections.

Full text queries

In Elasticsearch, full text queries reign supreme, enabling you to navigate your document kingdom with precision and finesse. They delve deep into the textual ocean, analyzing terms and weaving intricate search tapestries. With the match query as your trusty compass, you pinpoint specific words across fields, unearthing documents where your target resides. But your arsenal doesn't stop there! Multi-match queries stretch your reach, spanning multiple fields to uncover hidden gems. And for phrases that demand respect, the `phrase` and `phrase_prefix` queries stand guard, ensuring order and meaning stay intact. Beyond the match, Elasticsearch offers a smorgasbord of tools such as wildcards and fuzzy queries, handling typos and variations with grace.

For example, match and multi-match are great queries to implement for a full text search, so let's dig into them.

The match query

To uncover documents that align with a given text, number, date, or Boolean value, the match query is your go-to tool. It meticulously analyzes the provided input before initiating the matching process, making it the cornerstone of full text search in Elasticsearch. Notably, its capabilities extend to fuzzy matching, allowing flexibility in capturing relevant results.

For example, say we run the following query:

```
GET kibana_sample_data_ecommerce/_search
{
  "query": {
    "match": {
      "customer_first_name": "Eddie"
    }
  }
}
```

Here, we are doing a match query on the customer_first_name field in the index. The match query excels in full text search by meticulously analyzing your text input and constructing a Boolean query tailored to its nuances. It offers flexibility through the operator parameter, allowing you to choose between broader matches and/or stricter requirements. For even finer control, the minimum_should_match parameter empowers you to specify how many optional should clauses must be satisfied for a document to be considered a match. However, it is important to note that the parameters are only available when a new object is started within the query. My advice would be to include an example here:

```
GET kibana_sample_data_ecommerce/_search
{
  "query": {
    "match": {
      "customer_first_name": {
        "query": "this is a test",
        "operator": "and"
      }
    }
  }
}
```

The multi-match query

To expand your search beyond a single field, the multi_match query steps in. It inherits the strengths of the match query, empowering you to cast a wider net across multiple fields simultaneously, ensuring no relevant document goes undiscovered.

For example, consider the following query:

```
GET kibana_sample_data_ecommerce/_search
{
  "query": {
    "multi_match": {
      "query": "sweatshirt",
      "fields": ["products.product_name", "products.manufacturer"]
    }
  }
}
```

Here, we are searching for the word sweatshirt in two fields, namely product.product_name and category. This is great to use when the user is unsure of which exact field the keywords they are looking for can be found:

```
GET kibana_sample_data_ecommerce/_search
{
  "query": {
    "multi_match": {
      "query": "Sweatshirt",
      "fields": [
        "category.keyword",
        "products.manufacturer",
        "products.product_name^2" //field boosted by 2x
      ]
    }
  }
}
```

Here, if the word Sweatshirt is found in the products.product_name field, then the score for the respective document will be doubled. This helps the relevant documents to score higher and appear in the top documents in the result set.

Boosting effects can be summed up as the following:

- Documents with matches in boosted fields (products.product_name here) will rank higher in the results
- The higher the boost value, the stronger the influence on ranking

When left to its own devices, the multi_match query intelligently embraces a comprehensive approach. It consults the index.query.default_field setting, which typically defaults to encompassing all fields ripe for term queries while elegantly filtering out metadata fields. This results in a query that meticulously considers every relevant field, ensuring a thorough search experience.

The multi-match query can be of six different types, as explained in the following figure:

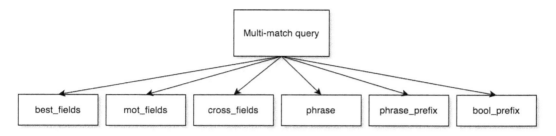

Figure 10.4 – The types of multi-match query in DSL queries

Let us learn about each of these multi-match query types:

- best_fields: This spotlights the most relevant match, prioritizing the field with the highest score while acknowledging matches in other fields

- most_fields: This champions inclusivity, considering matches in all fields and blending their scores to determine overall relevance

- cross_fields: This merges fields with harmonious analyzers into a virtual mega-field, enabling word-level matches across their collective expanse

- phrase: This preserves word order within individual fields, ensuring phrases such as ingest node aren't fragmented across separate fields

- phrase_prefix: This embraces flexibility, matching complete phrases or allowing for partial prefix matches within fields

- bool_prefix: This prioritizes prefix matches, ideal for scenarios such as autocomplete where initial characters hold the most significance

Geo queries

Users can unlock the power of location-based insights with Geo queries in Elasticsearch's Query DSL. These queries transform your data into a spatial playground, enabling you to uncover patterns and connections hidden within geographic coordinates. These can be further explained into different types as follows:

- geo-distance: This query works where you need to unearth documents within a specified distance of a given point. Imagine finding restaurants within 30 km (about 18.64 miles) of your current location or identifying potential customers within a delivery radius.

This can be tried with the following query:

```
GET kibana_sample_data_ecommerce/_search
{
  "query": {
    "geo_distance": {
      "distance": "30km",
      "geoip.location": {
        "lat": 20.0,
        "lon": 32.1
      }
    }
  }
}
```

Here, geoip.location is the geo field in Kibana's sample e-commerce index.

- geo-bounding: With this box query, you can enclose your search within a rectangular region, defining boundaries for exploration. Use it to filter events within a specific city or track assets within a designated area.

- geo-polygon: Users can embrace the irregular shapes with this query, allowing for more intricate geographic filtering. It is perfect for targeting customers within a specific sales territory or monitoring environmental conditions within a national park.

- geo-shape: You can now explore the full complexity of spatial data with this query, supporting various geometric shapes such as lines and circles. It is ideal for analyzing infrastructure networks, tracking natural phenomena, or exploring urban planning scenarios.

Shape queries

Shape queries unleash the power of geometric exploration within your data. These queries go beyond simple points and rectangles, allowing you to define and search for complex shapes, revealing spatial insights hidden within your Elasticsearch indices. Imagine analyzing intricate road networks with line queries, pinpointing environmental hazards within buffer zones using circle queries, or tracking the migratory patterns of endangered species with polygon queries. Shape queries handle them all!

Crafting a Shape query involves two key elements: defining the shape itself and specifying how it interacts with your indexed data. You can construct shapes directly within Kibana using intuitive drawing tools or upload pre-defined geometries in GeoJSON format.

Next, choose the relationship between your shape and the data. Intersects finds documents whose shapes overlap with yours, while Within identifies documents completely contained within your defined boundary. Contains flips the script, identifying documents that encompass your shape entirely.

And the flexibility doesn't stop there! Combine shapes with Boolean operators to create intricate search criteria. Imagine finding buildings both intersecting a flood zone and within a safe distance from a major fault line.

Shape queries aren't solely for visualization. They seamlessly integrate with aggregations, allowing you to count document occurrences within specific shapes, calculate statistics such as average area, or even analyze spatial relationships between multiple shapes. Whether you're a geospatial analyst, urban planner, or environmental scientist, Shape queries in Kibana empower you to delve deeper into your data, revealing a world of spatial insights waiting to be unearthed.

To see this query working on the ground, you need to have the appropriate field mapping and ensure that the data in that field is mapped. Let's look at an example:

1. We first create an employee index with the geo field called geometry and create the field mapping as shape:

    ```
    PUT /employee
    {
      "mappings": {
        "properties": {
          "geometry": {
            "type": "shape"
          }
        }
      }
    }
    ```

2. Next, we ingest a document with the relevant data in the geometry field:

    ```
    PUT /employee/_doc/1?refresh=wait_for
    {
      "name": "thegeolocation",
      "geometry": {
        "type": "point",
        "coordinates": [1355.400544, 5255.530286]
      }
    }
    ```

3. Next up, it is time to see the search doing its magic:

    ```
    GET /employee/_search
    {
      "query": {
        "shape": {
          "geometry": {
    ```

```
                    "shape": {
                      "type": "envelope",
                      "coordinates": [ [ 1354.0, 5354.0], [ 1401.0,
        5201.0] ]
                    },
                    "relation": "within"
                  }
                }
              }
            }
```

We have understood how we can create a geo mapping, ingest the data, and start running the queries that use the geo coordinates to help us search the points that come within the geo shape provided.

Joining queries

While joining data in the traditional relational sense isn't possible in Elasticsearch, Query DSL offers powerful alternatives to explore connections between documents. Forget clunky joins; embrace nested queries and parent-child relationships!

Nested queries let you embed documents within parent documents, creating hierarchical structures such as orders with their associated line items. Parent-child queries leverage dedicated fields to link documents, enabling you to search for parent documents based on their children's attributes, or vice versa. Imagine finding customers who placed orders exceeding a certain amount or identifying products frequently purchased together. These queries, while not true joins, offer efficient and flexible ways to navigate your data's interconnectedness, revealing hidden patterns and relationships that traditional searches might miss. Nested queries are a great example to understand how the joining of these queries works.

Nested query

To explore the intricate worlds nested within your documents, the nested query is your trusted guide. It acts as a portal, allowing you to search within nested fields as if they were independent documents, unearthing insights hidden within those complex structures.

Think of it as a magnifying glass, zooming in on specific objects within nested fields while keeping their connection to the parent document intact. When a match is found within a nested object, the nested query gracefully returns the entire parent document, ensuring you have the full context of the discovered information.

For example, refer to the following code:

```
PUT /sample
{
  "mappings": {
```

```
        "properties": {
            "first": {
                "type": "nested"
            }
        }
    }
}
```

Next, let's index a document in it:

```
PUT sample/_doc/1
{
    "group": "fans",
    "first": [
        {
            "pre": "sarah",
            "post":  "campion"
        },
        {
            "pre": "Tom",
            "post":  "wong"
        }
    ]
}
```

Finally, we can now search the documents using the nested query as follows:

```
GET sample/_search
{
    "query": {
        "nested": {
            "path": "first",
            "query": {
                "bool": {
                    "must": [
                        {"match": {"first.pre_1": "Tom"}},
                        {"match": {"first.post_2": "wong"}}
                    ]
                }
            }
        }
    }
}
```

This is how the nested query helps us to search through the data which can adopt the join functionality and thereby level up the search useability of the queries. It is important to take note that the performance is impacted by nested queries since the cluster has to process every nested pair as a new set of documents. Hence, the user needs to be mindful of this while implementing the nested queries.

Match-all queries

When you need to cast the widest net possible, embracing every document within your Elasticsearch index, the `match_all` query stands ready. It's a query of unparalleled simplicity, yet profound impact. It acts as a universal embrace, welcoming every document without discrimination, ensuring nothing is overlooked.

Think of it as a grand spotlight, illuminating every corner of your index, revealing the entirety of your data's landscape. When precision isn't the priority, but comprehensiveness reigns supreme, the `match_all` query is your steadfast ally.

Here is an example:

```
GET /_search
{
    "query": {
        "match_all": {}
    }
}
```

This helps us search through all the data present in the cluster through one JSON query.

Term-level queries

When you need pinpoint accuracy in your Elasticsearch searches, term-level queries are your precision instruments. They specialize in navigating structured data and effortlessly finding documents that match exact values within designated fields. Think of them as master codebreakers, effortlessly deciphering the secrets held within specific fields, such as dates, IP addresses, prices, and product IDs. Unlike full text queries that analyze and interpret language, term-level queries speak the language of precision. They bypass analysis and focus on exact matches, ensuring every character aligns perfectly with the stored data. When you need search results that leave no room for interpretation, term-level queries deliver certainty.

For example, the `exists` query is a type of term-level query that doesn't delve into the specific value of the field; it simply confirms its presence. This query shines when you need to identify documents with incomplete or missing data. It can expose patterns and anomalies that might otherwise go unnoticed.

Here is an example of it:

```
GET /_search
{
  "query": {
    "exists": {
      "city": "melbourne"
    }
  }
}
```

Here, `city` is a field and `melbourne` is the value that is being checked for whether it exists or not.

Specialized queries

Well, we've discussed queries enough. If you're tired of the same old search tricks, venture beyond the ordinary and unlock the hidden potential within your Kibana data with specialized queries. These unique tools go where others fear to tread, offering superpowers, which are stated in the following few examples:

- `percolate`: Turn the tables on traditional queries. With `percolate`, you store queries as documents, then let them hunt down matching documents. It's like setting a trap for the perfect search results, waiting for them to stumble into your digital snare.

- `Script_query`: Craft custom filters with the power of scripting. This query lets you write code to define your search criteria, opening a world of possibilities for tailored data exploration. It's like a magic spell for searching, conjuring up results that perfectly align with your unique needs.

- `Distance_feature`: Travel through time with this query, scoring documents based on their proximity to specific dates and even nanoseconds. It's like a time-traveling detective, sniffing out the closest matches with uncanny precision.

- `Rank_feature`: Unleash the power of numbers! `Rank_feature` scores documents based on their numeric features, making it ideal for prioritizing the most relevant results based on your custom criteria. It's like a data-driven judge, weighing each document's merit and handing you the top contenders.

- `More_like_this`: Find kindred spirits in your data! This query identifies documents such as your chosen text, document, or entire collections. Think of it as a literary matchmaker, connecting you with hidden gems that share your interests.

Compound queries

In Query DSL, compound queries act as masterful orchestrators, weaving together multiple queries to create intricate search symphonies. They embrace both leaf queries, those that search for specific values within fields, and other compound queries, effortlessly blending their strengths to achieve nuanced results. These queries offer three key abilities:

- **Combining results and scores**: Like master chefs blending flavors, compound queries artfully merge the outcomes of multiple queries, creating results richer than any single query could achieve. They expertly balance the scores of each contributing query, ensuring a harmonious final ranking.

- **Altering behavior**: Compound queries aren't content with merely combining results; they can also reshape the behavior of underlying queries. Imagine a chef adjusting a recipe's ingredients and enhancing certain flavors while muting others. Compound queries offer similar control, allowing you to fine-tune results to match your precise needs.

- **Switching contexts**: They can fluidly shift between query and filter contexts, each with distinct roles in search. Queries influence scores and relevance, while filters swiftly eliminate documents without affecting scores, like a precise sieve removing unwanted elements. Compound queries master this dance, ensuring each query type plays its part in perfect harmony.

For example, consider a Bool query. Imagine a master orchestrator, weaving together multiple melodies to create a symphony of search results. That's the essence of the Bool query, the heart of complex search logic in Elasticsearch.

Here's how it works:

- **Embracing diversity**: It gracefully combines diverse queries, whether they are simple leaf clauses or intricate compound queries, into a harmonious search experience.

- **Must-haves and possibilities**: It distinguishes between the must clauses, those essential for a match, and the should clauses, which add value but aren't mandatory. The more must and should clauses a document satisfies, the higher it ascends in the search results.

- **Non-negotiables and filters**: It asserts its authority with must_not clauses, excluding documents that dare to defy its criteria. For efficiency's sake, it employs filter clauses to swiftly eliminate unsuitable candidates early on.

By masterfully combining these elements, the Bool query empowers you to craft intricate search queries, ensuring only the most relevant and desired documents emerge from the depths of your Elasticsearch indices.

In this section, we explored in depth how DSL queries can be constructed from scratch, and how there is a range of queries to choose from to perform use-case-specific tasks. Now, let's move on to understanding the key management concept of Kibana – RBAC.

Deep-diving management concepts – RBAC

In the world of freely flowing data and insights, RBAC emerges as the vigilant gatekeeper, ensuring order and security amid the chaos.

Here's how it orchestrates harmony within your data domain:

- **Roles as blueprints**: RBAC defines distinct roles, each outlining a unique set of permissions, such as viewing specific dashboards, creating visualizations, or managing users.

- **Users and roles, linked in harmony**: Users are gracefully assigned to roles, aligning their access privileges with their responsibilities, ensuring sensitive information stays within authorized hands.

- **Spaces as fortresses**: We studied spaces in our earlier chapters. We can consider spaces as virtual realms where distinct teams or projects can collaborate safely. RBAC safeguards each space, controlling who can enter and what actions they can perform within those boundaries.

With RBAC as your trusty guardian, you can confidently share Kibana with diverse teams, fostering collaboration without compromising confidentiality. Sensitive data remains shielded, while authorized users explore and create with confidence.

Let's see a step-by-step process on how to implement RBAC in Kibana:

1. Access the **Stack Management** page. Navigate to the Kibana main menu (often represented by three horizontal lines):

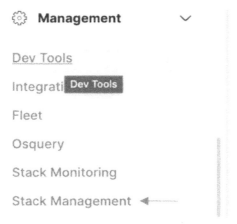

Figure 10.5 – Stack management navigation through the Kibana main menu

2.   Here, select **Security**, and click on **Roles**:

Figure 10.6 – Security | Roles under Stack Management in Kibana

3.   Then we create a new role; click the **Create role** button:

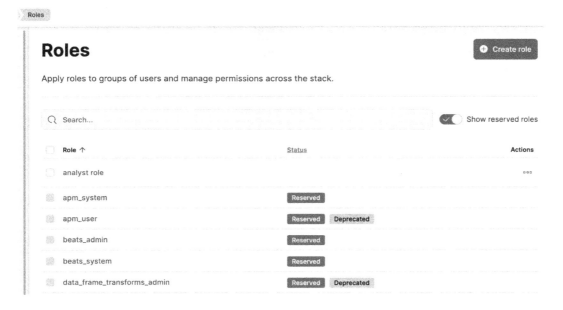

Figure 10.7 – The Create role button under Roles in Security

Give your role a descriptive name that reflects its purpose (for example, **Marketing_Analyst**).

For **Index privileges**, we can enter the data view that we need to give access to, for the user that has this role. Here, we are allowing access to the **kibana_sample_data_logs** data view:

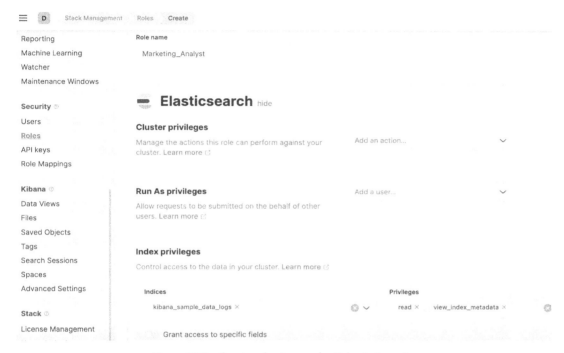

Figure 10.8 – Create role view under Roles in Security

You can leave **Cluster privileges** and **Run As privileges** empty. For **Index privileges**, we can enter the data view which we need to give access to, for the user that has this role.

4. Define **Permissions**. Carefully select the permissions that align with the role's responsibilities. Consider the following categories:

    *   **Spaces**: Control which spaces the role can access and what actions they can perform within those spaces.

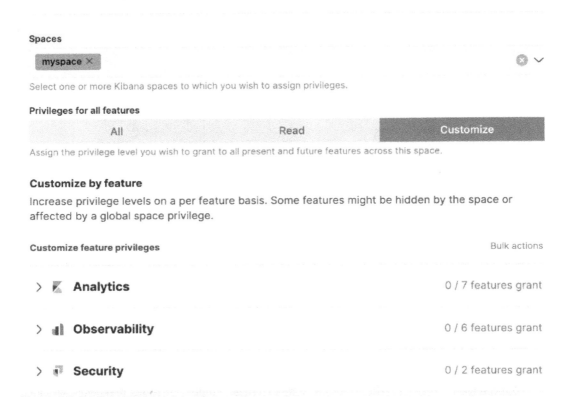

Kibana privileges

Spaces

myspace ✕

Select one or more Kibana spaces to which you wish to assign privileges.

Privileges for all features

All	Read	Customize

Assign the privilege level you wish to grant to all present and future features across this space.

Customize by feature

Increase privilege levels on a per feature basis. Some features might be hidden by the space or affected by a global space privilege.

Customize feature privileges   Bulk actions

> ⫶ **Analytics**   0 / 7 features grant

> ⫶ **Observability**   0 / 6 features grant

> ⫶ **Security**   0 / 2 features grant

Figure 10.9 – Space privileges under Roles in Security

- **Features**: Grant or restrict access to Kibana features such as dashboards, visualizations, alerts, and more. Here, we are allowing read access by selecting **Read** for **Dashboard** under **Analytics** and leaving all others as **None**, as seen in the following screenshot. This is to make sure that the user that has this role will only be able to read the dashboard of the allowed data views and nothing else in their Kibana view. How interesting!

Kibana privileges

Figure 10.10 – Features privilege in the Spaces | Create Role view

5. Assign users to the role. To do so, navigate to the **Users** tab within the **Security** section:

Figure 10.11 – The Users page navigation under Security in Stack Management

6.   Click the **Create user** button and navigate to the **Create user** page:

Figure 10.12 – The Create User button in Security, Stack Management

Enter the details as required: **User Name**: `analyst_user`, and **Password**: `public123`, would be unique to the respective user. Under **Roles**, select the newly created role from the list, which is **Marketing_Analytics** in this case.

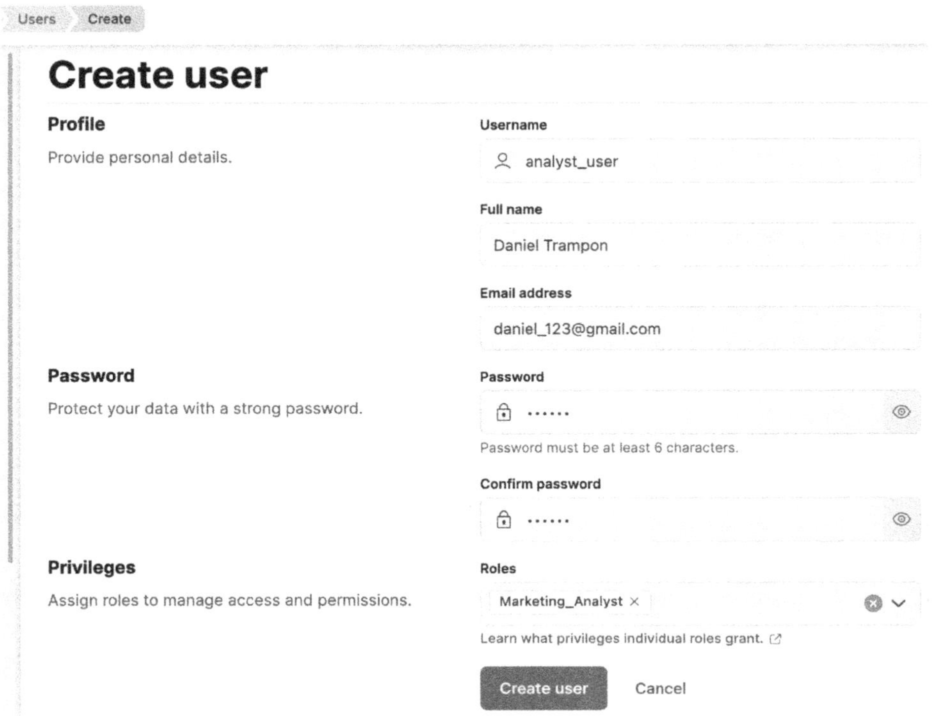

Figure 10.13 – The Create user view, Stack Management

Click on **Create user** to assign the role to the user.

7. Then we test and refine. Have a user with the assigned role log in to Kibana and verify that they can access the intended features and spaces, while restricted areas remain inaccessible.

For this purpose, log out of Kibana and log in again with the newly created credentials for `analyst_user`, and confirm whether the view of Kibana shows exactly according to the authorization we had set up in the **Roles** section. By doing so, we can say that by setting roles, we set up the authorization for the user and control what they can access, while, by setting users, we set up authentication, which helps us control the access to Kibana and thereby control the access to our data and Elasticsearch cluster. We can illustrate this in the following figure:

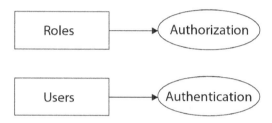

Figure 10.14 – Concept of RBAC

Additionally, you can leverage Kibana's built-in roles for common use cases as a starting point and create a naming convention for roles to maintain clarity and organization.

It is a good idea to regularly review and update roles as your security needs and user base evolve.

In this section, we learned how to implement RBAC and the importance of the implementation, which extends to providing security to the sensitive data in the workspace. Let's climb the ladder further and understand how we get notified about an important event through watchers.

Exploring watchers

It has been a very essential need of the hour to stay on top of critical changes that can feel like chasing butterflies in a hurricane. Kibana presents you with a valiant ally: watchers. These vigilant guardians stand guard over your Elasticsearch indices, tirelessly monitoring for pre-defined conditions and triggering actions the moment they're met.

Think of watchers as automated sentries patrolling your data fortress. They meticulously comb through indices, searching for specific events, metric thresholds, or even unusual deviations in data patterns. And when they encounter their quarry, they spring into action!

The way they function is impressive:

- **Triggering alerts**: They notify you via email, SMS, or other channels about crucial developments, ensuring you stay informed even when away from Kibana

- **Running actions**: They execute pre-defined scripts or workflows, such as automatically adjusting configurations, triggering downstream processes, or even sending help desk tickets when issues arise

The possibilities are endless! Imagine watchers doing the following:

- Alerting you when server temperatures spike, potentially preventing hardware failure

- Notifying marketing of sudden shifts in website traffic, allowing them to capitalize on trending topics

- Triggering an automated incident response when suspicious activity is detected in your network

With watchers vigilantly guarding your data, you can rest assured that no critical event will slip through the cracks. You'll receive timely alerts, initiate automated responses, and ultimately gain a deeper understanding of your data's dynamic landscape. Time to take an example of how these watchers can be useful in a real market scenario.

Imagine you're the lead engineer of a bustling e-commerce platform during a massive holiday sale. Orders are pouring in and the excitement is palpable. But amid the chaos, you know that even a momentary downtime could spell disaster. That's where watchers step in to ensure smooth sailing.

You create a watcher named `Holiday Hero` with the following tasks:

- **Monitor key metrics**: Watchfully observe server response times, database query rates, and error logs for any signs of strain. Track inventory levels of popular items to prevent frustrating out-of-stock situations.

- **Trigger timely alerts**: Notify the on-call team immediately via email and SMS if any metric exceeds its threshold, allowing for swift intervention.

    Send alerts to the marketing team when inventory levels dip, enabling them to adjust promotions or highlight alternative products.

- **Initiate automated actions**: Automatically scale server resources proactively to handle increased traffic, ensuring a seamless customer experience.

    Temporarily disable non-essential features to reduce server load during peak periods.

As the sale progresses, `Holiday Hero` proves its worth:

- It catches a sudden spike in server response times early on, prompting the team to allocate additional resources before any customers experience delays

- It alerts the marketing team to a dwindling stock of a popular item, leading to a timely social media campaign highlighting similar products, which prevents lost sales

- It detects a potential security breach attempt and automatically blocks the offending IP addresses, safeguarding customer data and preventing further attacks

Thanks to the vigilant watcher, the sale concludes as a resounding success. Customers are delighted with the smooth shopping experience, and the team breathes a collective sigh of relief, knowing they've averted potential crises and secured a happy holiday season for everyone involved. Sounds promising? Let's see how to set up a watcher by following these steps:

1. You will need to navigate to **Watcher**. Open the Kibana menu (typically three horizontal lines) and select **Stack Management**:

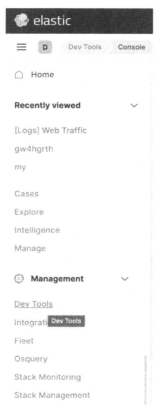

Figure 10.15 – Navigation to Stack Management, Kibana

2. Define the trigger. Navigate to **Watcher** under **Alerts and Insights**.

Alerts and Insights ⓘ

Rules

Cases

Connectors

Reporting

Machine Learning

Watcher

Mainte indows

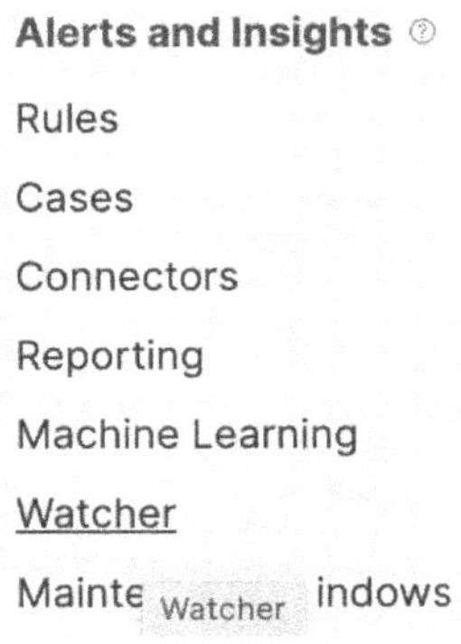

Figure 10.16 – Watcher under Alerts and Insights

3. Click on **Create**:

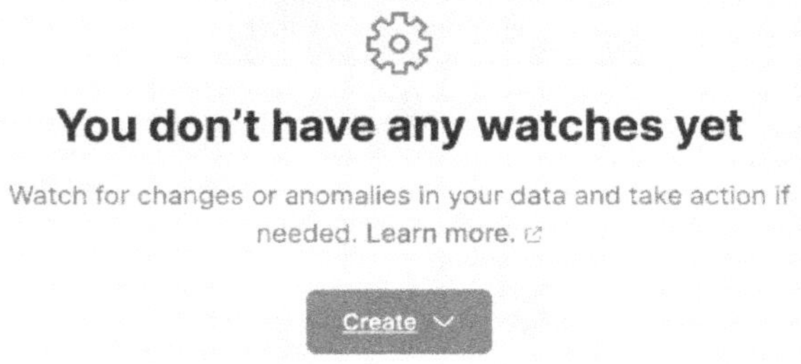

You don't have any watches yet

Watch for changes or anomalies in your data and take action if
needed. Learn more. ⤢

Figure 10.17 – The Create button for watchers

4. Next, we can set two types of alerts, as shown here. For this case, let's go with **Create threshold alert**:

Create threshold alert
Send an alert on a specified condition.

Create advanced watch
Set up a custom watch in JSON.

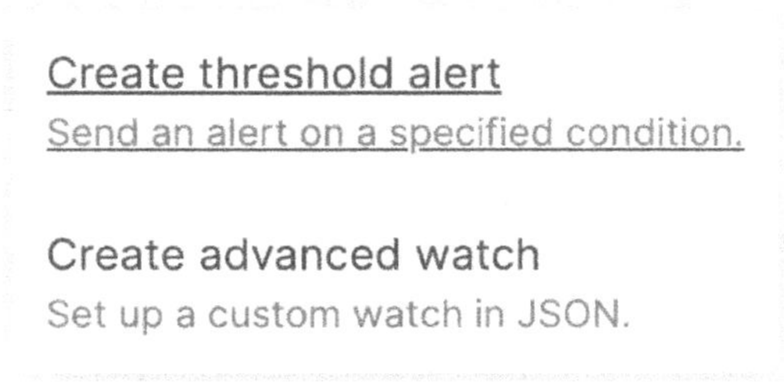

Figure 10.18 – Selection of the types of watchers

5. In the next step, give your watcher a descriptive name and choose its **Indices to query** and **Time field**. Also, define the condition that triggers the watcher. For example, this could be as defined as follows:

Figure 10.19 – The creation of a watcher

Condition: For example, the alert will be triggered when the average of **bytes** is above 8,000 for the last one day. The graph created below the condition rightly depicts the trend of such instances that happened in history.

6. Craft the actions. Choose the actions to execute when the trigger fires. You can send notifications and alert via email, SMS, Slack, or other channels, as shown here:

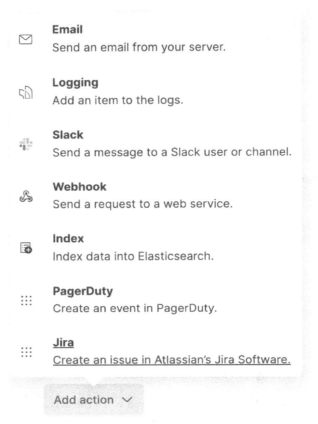

Email

Send an email from your server.

Logging

Add an item to the logs.

Slack

Send a message to a Slack user or channel.

Webhook

Send a request to a web service.

Index

Index data into Elasticsearch.

PagerDuty

Create an event in PagerDuty.

Jira

Create an issue in Atlassian's Jira Software.

Add action ∨

Figure 10.20 – The selection of the action to be executed upon the watcher trigger

For this example, let's go with **Index**, where we store the alert trigger information in an Elasticsearch index named **runtime_watch_index** for further analysis.

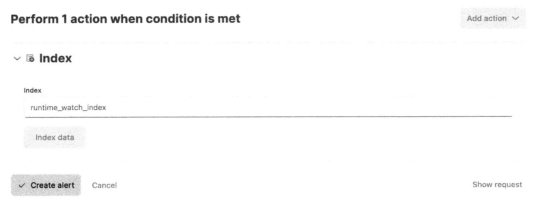

Perform 1 action when condition is met   Add action ∨

∨ 🗔 **Index**

Index

runtime_watch_index

Index data

✓ Create alert   Cancel   Show request

Figure 10.21 – Selection of the Index option as the action

Once done, select **Create alert** and the job is done. The watcher now gets activated.

7. Then we test and refine as required. You can then run a test trigger to verify its functionality and monitor the watcher's execution history, and adjust actions or triggers as needed.

In this section, we explored in detail how we can automate the process of notifying the audience about any noteworthy events that could happen in the data analysis through watchers. Note that the process steps stated in the preceding example are just the basic steps. Depending on your specific needs and triggers, the configuration can become more complex.

Summary

This chapter takes a deep dive into the potent tools that empower you to navigate and refine your data within Elasticsearch through Kibana. It opens with Query DSL, your trusty language for crafting intricate search queries, unearthing specific insights hidden within your Elasticsearch indices. You'll master queries that pinpoint exact values, analyze full text, and even explore intricate shapes within your data.

Next, it introduces Kibana RBAC, the vigilant gatekeeper safeguarding your data domain. By tailoring roles and permissions, you ensure sensitive information stays secure while fostering collaboration within designated spaces. We learned how to create roles, assign users, and watch as RBAC orchestrates a harmonious balance between access and security.

Finally, the chapter unveils the power of watchers, your automated sentinels tirelessly monitoring your data fortress. We've discovered how to define triggers that react to critical events, triggering alerts, executing actions, and transforming your data from a passive observer to a proactive guardian. This comprehensive chapter equips you with the essential tools to unlock the full potential of the features, empowering you to explore, secure, and react to your data with precision and clarity.

Congratulations! You've navigated the labyrinthine world of Kibana, emerging triumphant with data analysis superpowers. You can now wrangle your Elasticsearch indices like a digital cowboy, lassoing insights with your masterful Query DSL, herding dashboards into beautiful visualizations, and even commanding watchers to stand guard against data droughts. But remember, this is just the beginning of your data exploration journey. Think of Kibana as your trusty steed, ready to gallop through terabytes of information. So, saddle up, data wrangler, and let your inner analyst run wild! Just be careful not to fall into the rabbit hole of endless graphs and charts – remember, there's a whole world outside your screen filled with sunshine, puppies, and (dare I say it?) non-numerical adventures. So, go forth, analyze with confidence, and let your data analysis skills shine brighter than a million pie charts combined. Just promise you won't use your new knowledge to predict the winning numbers at the next lottery – some things are best left to the mysteries of the universe (or Excel, whichever you prefer).

Happy analyzing, fellow data explorer! May your dashboards be beautiful, your queries efficient, and your insights always surprising (except when they're not because data can be like that sometimes).

P.S. If you ever get lost in the Kibana jungle, don't worry, there's a whole community of friendly data enthusiasts ready to guide you back. Just remember, the only silly question is the one you don't ask (unless it's "Why is there a pie chart of cat memes?" Then maybe just keep that one to yourself).

Index

W

www.packtpub.com

Subscribe to our online digital library for full access to over 7,000 books and videos, as well as industry leading tools to help you plan your personal development and advance your career. For more information, please visit our website.

Why subscribe?

- Spend less time learning and more time coding with practical eBooks and Videos from over 4,000 industry professionals
- Improve your learning with Skill Plans built especially for you
- Get a free eBook or video every month
- Fully searchable for easy access to vital information
- Copy and paste, print, and bookmark content

Did you know that Packt offers eBook versions of every book published, with PDF and ePub files available? You can upgrade to the eBook version at packtpub.com and as a print book customer, you are entitled to a discount on the eBook copy. Get in touch with us at customercare@packtpub.com for more details.

At www.packtpub.com, you can also read a collection of free technical articles, sign up for a range of free newsletters, and receive exclusive discounts and offers on Packt books and eBooks.

Other Books You May Enjoy

If you enjoyed this book, you may be interested in these other books by Packt:

Getting Started with Elastic Stack 8.0

Asjad Athick

ISBN: 9781800569492

- Configure Elasticsearch clusters with different node types for various architecture patterns
- Ingest different data sources into Elasticsearch using Logstash, Beats, and Elastic Agent
- Build use cases on Kibana including data visualizations, dashboards, machine learning jobs, and alerts
- Design powerful search experiences on top of your data using the Elastic Stack
- Secure your organization and learn how the Elastic SIEM and Endpoint Security capabilities can help
- Explore common architectural considerations for accommodating more complex requirements

Machine Learning with the Elastic Stack

Rich Collier, Camilla Montonen, Bahaaldine Azarmi

ISBN: 9781801070034

- Find out how to enable the ML commercial feature in the Elastic Stack
- Understand how Elastic machine learning is used to detect different types of anomalies and make predictions
- Apply effective anomaly detection to IT operations, security analytics, and other use cases
- Utilize the results of Elastic ML in custom views, dashboards, and proactive alerting
- Train and deploy supervised machine learning models for real-time inference
- Discover various tips and tricks to get the most out of Elastic machine learning

Packt is searching for authors like you

If you're interested in becoming an author for Packt, please visit `authors.packtpub.com` and apply today. We have worked with thousands of developers and tech professionals, just like you, to help them share their insight with the global tech community. You can make a general application, apply for a specific hot topic that we are recruiting an author for, or submit your own idea.

Share your thoughts

Now you've finished *Kibana 8.x: A Quick Start Guide to Data Analysis*, we'd love to hear your thoughts! Scan the QR code below to go straight to the Amazon review page for this book and share your feedback or leave a review on the site that you purchased it from.

`https://packt.link/r/1803232161`

Your review is important to us and the tech community and will help us make sure we're delivering excellent quality content.

Download a free PDF copy of this book

Thanks for purchasing this book!

Do you like to read on the go but are unable to carry your print books everywhere?

Is your eBook purchase not compatible with the device of your choice?

Don't worry, now with every Packt book you get a DRM-free PDF version of that book at no cost.

Read anywhere, any place, on any device. Search, copy, and paste code from your favorite technical books directly into your application.

The perks don't stop there, you can get exclusive access to discounts, newsletters, and great free content in your inbox daily

Follow these simple steps to get the benefits:

1. Scan the QR code or visit the link below

https://packt.link/free-ebook/9781803232164

2. Submit your proof of purchase
3. That's it! We'll send your free PDF and other benefits to your email directly

www.ingramcontent.com/pod-product-compliance
Lightning Source LLC
Chambersburg PA
CBHW080528060326
40690CB00022B/5065